Peter Seitz
Designing a Life

Peter Seitz
Designing a Life

Minneapolis College of Art & Design
Minneapolis, Minnesota

Contents

Foreword

Michael O'Keefe
President, Minneapolis College
of Art and Design

The history of modern design, as with any major cultural movement, is the accumulation of the contributions and leadership of numerous individuals. This book, *Peter Seitz: Designing a Life*, is the story of one such individual, a designer who was both pivotal in shaping modern design as well as crucial to bringing that movement to the Upper Midwest. The Walker Art Center, the Minneapolis College of Art and Design (MCAD), and numerous design firms and advertising agencies have been on the cutting edge of design for years, in part, because of Peter Seitz's grounding in modernism, his convictions about design, and where he found himself as a practicing professional.

Peter's role as a teacher began at the Maryland Institute College of Art in Baltimore, where he spent two years before embarking on a new journey that would ultimately reshape the design landscape of Minnesota. In 1964, Peter came to Minneapolis to become design curator at the Walker Art Center. With this move, the strands of modern design—from its European origins to its first expressions on the East Coast—came together in what Andrew Blauvelt in his essay calls the "grassroots spread of modernism" and its ideals across the United States.

Peter arrived in the Twin Cities at around the same time that Rob Roy Kelly became the first design chair at the Minneapolis College of Art and Design, bringing to this college, via Yale, the European tradition of design education. The arrival on the Minneapolis scene of these two practitioners of modern design also coincided with the beginning of what has been a hallmark of this community ever since: a healthy commitment on the part of business leaders to culture, the arts, and good design. The confluence of interest in modern design in the for-profit and nonprofit sectors, in turn, spawned highly creative advertising, graphic arts, and design businesses that flourish to this day.

In his interview with Kolean Pitner, Peter discusses his ethos of work and the mandate to support community, themes that appeared throughout his life as a practicing designer and teacher. Bruce N. Wright focuses on his professional practice: Peter the institution builder, the community champion, the consummate leader. In his essay, Blauvelt explores the significance of Peter as an émigré to the Midwest, an importer of international modernism.

Central to Peter's life is his conviction that professional practice must include dedication to future generations of practitioners. His advocacy included a commitment to teaching while working full-time in each of the many firms he founded. As Kolean outlines in her essay, his contributions to the profession, whether upholding his design principles, establishing productive businesses, or championing professional organizations such as the Minnesota Graphic Design Association (now the Minnesota chapter of the American Institute of Graphic Arts), the Community Design Center, and the Association for Computing Machinery's Special Interest Group on Graphics and Interactive Techniques (SIGGRAPH), include lasting and significant contributions to design education.

Peter taught at MCAD from 1971 to 2002, and when he tried to retire in the mid-1990s, we called him back to be acting chair of the Design Department. He created the first computer lab at MCAD, now an integral component of all visual arts programs. Peter brought a vision to the college that launched new technologies and gave us a rigorous foundation in the European fine arts tradition and in methods specific to design. As a teacher and mentor, he has left a legacy of successful leaders in design and advertising as well as other creative disciplines. We at MCAD—including those many alumni who benefited—are grateful for his role in the development of our internationally recognized design program. By the luck of circumstance, Peter, an Ulm native son, became our Minnesota local hero.

There is much inspiration to be gained from reflection on the life of this productive man. He says it well for all of us: "Design your life." We have taken heed. Peter's path is an example of what can happen when opportunity meets preparedness, strong intent, and a disciplined approach to experience and practice as well as an acceptance of all that life might throw our way. We, the inheritors of his leadership, and the many students whose lives he has affected, owe a debt of gratitude to him for what he has given us: Peter Seitz, your community applauds you.

Acknowledgments

Pam Arnold
Director of DesignWorks,
Minneapolis College of Art
and Design

"Little, but all roses!" as the poet Sappho is quoted to have inveighed. This project simply called on the best, and there are many talented people to thank.

First we extend our deepest appreciation to our authors Kolean Pitner and Bruce N. Wright, whose passion about Peter Seitz's life and work made this possible for all of us. To Vince Leo, Vice President of Academic Affairs at the Minneapolis College of Art and Design (MCAD), who found the seed money to help make this project a reality and who gave DesignWorks the legs to carry the project forward, and to Mike O'Keefe, President of MCAD, for honoring our passion for it and for supporting the project, we are extremely grateful.

I have no illusions that the quality of this book is the result of anything other than the magic of brilliant collaborations. Andrew Blauvelt, Design Director and Curator at the Walker Art Center, is a designer and person of the highest order. His oversight of the project demonstrated his bottomless work ethic and humble compassion. Life is short, but a colleague like Andrew makes it ever so sweet. Under his wing is Ryan Nelson, the designer of this book, who accepted the project as a student at MCAD and senior designer in the college's studio, DesignWorks. While working on the book, Ryan interviewed for graduate school at the Werkplaats Typografie in the Netherlands and for a design fellowship at the Walker. As luck would have it, he accepted the position at the Walker. Ryan is destined for success as a brilliant designer. How extraordinary that this book to honor Peter Seitz is designed and produced by two such capable heirs to his professional legacy.

Joe Avery at Shapco, our printer, worked with us to craft a beautiful object. Pamela Johnson responded to the call with her superb editorial attention to detail. So many others also helped put us on our path: Jim Madson, the staff at AIGA MN, and the many friends who advised us. At the Walker Art Center Library and Archives, Jill Vuchetich, Daniel Smith, and Barb Economan provided access to important materials. Photographers Patrick Kelley, Gene Pittman, Rik Sferra, and Cameron Wittig helped us document Peter's life and work, and Greg Beckel insured that the book's images would reproduce beautifully.

A special thanks to Peter's friends and colleagues who provided important documents, stories, and insights. Peter's former students and MCAD colleagues—Monica Little, Todd Nesser, Charles Spencer Anderson, Jerry Stenback, Jo Davison, Peter Chan, Kristen McDougall, Russ Mroczek, Kevin Byrne, Hazel Gamec, and Carol (Stenborg) Zen, and myself shared design education experiences. Tim Larsen, Dale Johnston, Jim Johnson, Eric Madsen, Miranda Moss, Dick Mueller, Heather Olson, and Ken Resen reflected on Peter's contributions to the professional design community. Duane Thorbeck generously shared his InterDesign archives and memories as did Roger B. Martin and InterDesign "alumni" Jim Dustrude, Sandy Stein, Damon Farber, and Neal Libson. Roger Clemence contributed his enthusiasm and notes about the beginnings of the Community Design Center and its social importance. Gay Beste Reineck offered wonderful stories of working for Peter at the Walker and at InterDesign.

Much appreciation to MCAD, to everyone at the college who shows up every day for art and design education, and to the MCAD development team who fight the good fight for ensuring that we have scholarships for worthy students.

I'm delighted that we could produce the book to coincide with the thirtieth anniversary of the founding of AIGA Minnesota, whose existence was predicated on the formation of the Minnesota Graphic Design Association, which—like so many other things—Peter had a hand in shaping.

To thank Peter is a gross understatement of gratitude. This book is really a small gesture, but hopefully will be received by him as all roses. Peter stands for the founders of this region's creative economy who have given the Twin Cities its reputation for excellence. Peter, you have made a community of professionals, and friends.

Finally, we acknowledge all professionals who honor the future by electing to teach, and thereby become students again themselves.

Designing a Life

Peter Seitz at his home in Pepin, Wisconsin, 2007

A Conversation with Peter Seitz

Interviewed by Kolean Pitner, design historian and faculty member, College of Visual Arts, St. Paul

The story of design pioneer Peter Seitz is part of our history as a design community. The following conversation is culled from a series of extensive interviews conducted after Seitz's induction as Minnesota's first AIGA Fellow in 2000. It offers insight not only into his background and his philosophy of design and of life, but also the greater historical and cultural context in which the graphic design profession developed in the state. His memories, and those of his colleagues, together help form the building blocks of the Minnesota design community's collective experience.

Kolean Pitner (KP): To begin at the beginning, tell us about your childhood in Germany. Who were some of the people who influenced you to pursue a career as a graphic designer? Peter Seitz (PS): Growing up, I didn't think about graphic design because I didn't know it existed, but I did like drawing, painting, and reading illustrated books. Although our family was poor and life in Germany was very stressful during the rise of the Nazi Party before World War II, my mother encouraged my artistic interests. I developed a passionate interest in the United States by reading a series of Wild West novels by German author Karl May (1842–1912). These legendary tales about a noble Indian named Winnetou and his German blood brother Old Shatterhand completely captivated my imagination.[1] These books, which I checked out of the local library over and over again, were a great escape from the war clouds that were developing all around us. During the summers, my brothers and I spent our time working at our father's family farm, five miles northwest of Schwabmünchen,

1. Karl May's *Winnetou* adventure novels, which have sold more than 100 million copies, have significantly shaped the way many Europeans view the American frontier. See Danica Tutush, "The Strange Life and Legacy of Karl May," *Cowboys & Indians* (September 1999).

Germany, where we lived. This 65-acre dairy and wheat farm was run by our two aunts and two uncles—all four of whom were unmarried. They introduced us to the rigors of farm life in hopes that one of us would take to farming and eventually take over operation of the farm. One of the first things I learned was that I didn't want to be a farmer! KP: How did the war directly affect your family? PS: My father was drafted into the German army in early 1944. Just over a year later on a snowy Sunday morning (March 4, 1945), Schwabmünchen was bombed. I remember that my brother Wolfgang and I were playing outside in the snow when we heard the sirens. As we ran home, we heard the planes overhead. Fortunately, we made it to our basement before the bombs fell.[2] I was thirteen and had not yet finished the eighth grade when the war ended three months later. But because the two schools had been destroyed and my parents could not afford to send me away to school, I was apprenticed to a local master painter, the respected craftsman Herr Luipold Gogl. From him I learned sign painting and how to paint wood and imitate hardwood grain patterns with precision.[3] This is where I learned the importance of quality craftsmanship, the basic elements of lettering and the value of hard work. At this time, I also went to Augsburg once a month for classroom instruction in this craft. I particularly liked and excelled at hand lettering. After three years of working and studying, I became a journeyman painter and diligently worked at my trade for five years. I also realized that this was not what I wanted to do for the rest of my life. KP: Did you know what you wanted to do as a career? When did you discover graphic design? PS: A turning point came in 1953, when one of my friends introduced me to a talented graphic designer who had graduated from the art school in Augsburg. He worked for the Augsburg opera house, where he designed all its printed promotional materials. When I saw his work, I was awestruck. I thought this guy has the best job in the world! Right then and there, I knew I wanted to be a graphic designer. I began my design studies at Augsburg in 1954. Herr Eugene Nerdinger, director of the graphic arts department, was also a noted calligrapher and author. I guess he was impressed with my drive and work ethic because he recommended me for a part-time job as a production artist at a local textile-engraving company.[4] This job helped me to expand my knowledge of the graphic arts and to better understand printing processes. KP: How did you get from art school in Augsburg to Ulm? PS: Chance intervened. One Sunday morning in July 1955, when I was with my parents, my mother showed me an article in the Schwabmünchen newspaper about a school of design that had recently opened its new campus just outside Ulm. It was a glowing summary about the start-up year at the Hochschule für Gestaltung Ulm (HfG Ulm), and how it was continuing the modernist ideals taught at the famous German design school, the Bauhaus. The article quoted Walter Gropius, the first Bauhaus director, and his former student Max Bill (a Swiss architect, designer, and painter), who was the first director of HfG Ulm. I couldn't believe such an amazing school existed! It was nearby, and they were recruiting students. The next day I rode my bicycle sixty miles to Ulm to

2. The bombs (272 firebomb bundles of 500 pounds each) were slightly off target due to poor weather conditions and narrowly missed the Seitz house, which was located near the edge of town. More than 100 buildings were completely destroyed, including the government building, the Catholic church, two schools, and several factories. 3. In Germany and all across Europe during this time, only the wealthy could afford hardwood furniture. Most pieces were made of inexpensive softwood hand-painted with hardwood grain patterns to resemble the more expensive material. 4. Textile engraving is the reproduction of decorative design onto fabric via the engraving printing process. Seitz had the exacting job of painting color separations onto acetates that were then etched into repeats on copper cylinders.

check out the campus and ask about enrolling as a design student in the fall. Strikingly situated on a hill overlooking the Danube River, I was immediately struck by the stunningly beautiful modernist architecture and how the campus was completely set apart from the city of Ulm. I later found out that its isolated setting was an intentional part of the school's philosophy. It reinforced a cloisterlike environment in which students and teachers studied together without distraction. Max Bill wanted us to focus on solving the design problems of industrial societies. He often said, "We want our students to participate in the making of a new culture, from spoon to city." But I'm getting ahead of myself. Fortunately for me, the school was looking for more mature students who had not been educated in traditional European universities. They were particularly interested in skilled craftsmen. So after completing the application process and showing my portfolio, I was accepted as a first year student for the autumn of 1955. I was a twenty-four-year-old freshman!   KP: Tell us more about why attending HfG Ulm was such a turning point for you. Looking back, how did it change the direction of your life? PS: Attending HfG Ulm had a profound impact on the direction of my life. I had never been exposed to such a diverse and highly skilled group of people (both faculty and students).[5] I knew I had been given an incredible educational opportunity. I loved my classes, but I have to admit that my favorite thing that first year was having indoor plumbing for the first time. Access to flushing toilets and being able to take a hot shower anytime of the day or night were luxuries beyond anything I had ever experienced. Reading that newspaper article about the opening of the school was chance, luck, or whatever you want to call it. The important thing is that I recognized that it was an important opportunity and decided to act on it. Since then, my philosophy of life has been that you should actively make your own decisions rather than passively having decisions made for you. That's how I have designed my life. I have aimed at things and have moved toward them in a way that made it possible for them to happen. I didn't make them happen, but I put myself in their way. I had to work for them, talk to people—lots of different people—try different communication methods, and explore new avenues.   KP: The Ulm curriculum, like the Bauhaus, had an amazing influence on art and design education around the world. What was it like to be a part of this visionary approach to education? PS: Truly inspiring! Like I said before, HfG Ulm was modeled after the great German design school the Bauhaus, which was shut down by the Nazis in 1933. The underlying educational idea at the Bauhaus and at Ulm was to unify all of the visual arts so we could make the world better through art and design. An interdisciplinary approach to design was at the heart of the curriculum. The three main departments—architecture, visual communications, and product design—collaborated on a variety of projects during the foundation course, which was a full year of basic design studies that all first-year students took. Afterward, each student focused on his or her particular area of interest. Mine, of course, was visual communications, which was the term used for graphic design.

5. During the period that Seitz attended HfG Ulm, each freshman class was composed of 30 to 35 students and the total student population ranged from 120 to 140, of which 40 to 50 percent were foreign students, primarily from neighboring European countries, the United States, and Japan.

The goal of the overall curriculum was to teach us to be highly qualified designers with a deep commitment to social and cultural responsibility.[6] We were taught that design is not frivolous; it is serious. Good design is very serious. Inventive, but serious. Argentine designer Tomás Maldonado, one of my foundation course teachers, also became one of my mentors. During my senior year, he encouraged me to consider teaching design sometime during my career as a graphic designer.   KP: Tell us about more about your teachers. Which ones were most influential? Why? PS: During my second year, I had the opportunity to work on two projects with Max Bill. This was at a time when a philosophical rift had developed between "the old guard" of Bill and his supporters and "the new guard" of faculty and students who wanted to develop a more scientific and technological approach to design. After all of the political infighting, Max Bill resigned. Because I was one of his supporters, I lost my scholarship. As a result, the next two years were financially very difficult. In my third and fourth years of study, Otl Aicher taught the specialized graphic design courses. I admired everything about him—his design skills, his lifestyle (witty, sophisticated, and always well dressed), and his positive personality. He was a devoted teacher and I learned so much from him. He asked me to work in his design studio and became my most influential mentor. Another important person in my life at that time was an American student from the Minneapolis School of Art [now the Minneapolis College of Art and Design], John Lottes, who was studying at Ulm on a Fulbright Scholarship.[7] We became friends, and I practiced my English (not very good at the time) with him. He often talked about his life in the United States and piqued my interest in American culture. For the first time, I considered traveling abroad.   KP: So how did you make the leap from Ulm to Yale University? PS: In 1958, Otl Aicher spent six weeks teaching and lecturing at Yale. When he returned, he encouraged me to apply to the Yale School of Art and Architecture graduate program. So I did. I also applied for a Fulbright Scholarship, which I didn't get. But I was a runner-up and received a $250 travel grant from the American Women's Club at the Stuttgart Army Base. It may not seem like much now, but it was a princely sum at the time. It was all the money I had when I came to America. Because I became sick during my last term at Ulm, it took me extra time to complete my thesis (a corporate identity for Hubert Fisheries in Hamburg, Germany [pages 92 and 93]). It was late summer when I finished the design project. I had to finish writing the thesis during my first semester at Yale. At the same time, I was desperate to find a way to America. Flying was too expensive, so I asked everyone I knew for suggestions. Walter Zeischegg, a product design teacher at Ulm, contacted a friend and arranged for me to have free passage on a Danish freighter from Hamburg to Montreal. The only problem was that it meant that I wouldn't arrive in New Haven until several days after classes had started. But it was my only option and I took it.   KP: That must have been stressful journey. How did it all work out? PS: You have to understand that for a German to be late for school was an unthinkable transgression. I was afraid they would send me

6. For more information about HfG Ulm, which operated from 1954 to 1968, see Herbert Lindinger, ed., *Ulm Design: The Morality of Objects*, trans. David Britt (Cambridge, Massachusetts: MIT Press, 1991).   7. Seitz and Lottes met again years later in Minneapolis when Lottes became president of the Society of Fine Arts, the governing board of the Minneapolis Institute of Arts.

back home. But it turned out to be a blessing. Alvin Eisenman, the head of the design department, arranged for me to stay in a room at the International Center. My roommate was Richard Jolly, a law student from Cambridge, England. He was very kind and helped me to speak English. Although I felt one step behind at the beginning of the first semester, I did catch up and made progress in all of my classes.   KP: When you began your graduate studies at the prestigious graphic design program at Yale, celebrated graphic designers Paul Rand, Bradbury Thompson, and Herbert Matter were your teachers. Tell us about that educational experience. PS: I was completely intimidated by Paul Rand, especially since my English skills were still rather limited. I couldn't explain my designs, which put me in a difficult position. He was very tough. His students dubbed him "the curmudgeon." But, still, he was an excellent teacher. He taught me how to think about the essence of a piece. I hated his harsh critiques, but ended up respecting him. Like so many of my visiting professors at Yale, Bradbury Thompson was a professional designer as well as a gifted instructor. He taught typography and publication design, while his work ranged from innovative publication design for the paper company Westvaco Corporation (*Westvaco Inspirations*) to the inspirational and brilliantly designed *Washburn College Bible*. He was a gentleman designer and teacher, imparting his love for the history of type and typography as well as all the arts. I also took photography classes from Herbert Matter, the pioneering Swiss designer and photographer. I enjoyed photography so much that I told Alvin Eisenman I wanted to switch from graphic design to photography, but he knew I was too self-conscious to do what professional photographers had to do to succeed. He said, "No," and that was that.   KP: Were there internship opportunities available to Yale graduate students at that time? PS: Yes. After my first year of graduate school in 1960, I had a summer internship with the McCann Erickson advertising agency in New York City. Based on that experience, I discovered that I didn't want to be an art director. I wanted and needed to be a designer. I thought my dream job would be to work in a museum. So when Martin Friedman from the Walker Art Center in Minneapolis came to interview second-year graduate students for a design director and curator position, I was thrilled. Although Martin said he was very interested in hiring me, the board of directors decided the museum didn't have the funds for any new positions at that particular time. By my second year, I had adjusted to my new life and began to enjoy myself. I still had to work hard to make ends meet, but it didn't seem quite so difficult to do now. I worked on my thesis (a series of theater posters) and graduated in the top third of my class.[8]   KP: Did you have any job prospects when you graduated? PS: Since I didn't want to go back to the ad agency, I walked the streets of New York City with my portfolio, just like most graduate students. I applied for a job at the Museum of Modern Art, but they weren't hiring. Six weeks later, I was hired by the architectural firm of I.M. Pei and Associates. Pei's office was one of the first to include a graphic design department within a large architectural and urban-planning practice. The function of the graphic design department was to

8. For more information about Yale's graduate school program in graphic design during the 1950s and 1960s, see Rob Roy Kelly, "The Early Years of Graphic Design at Yale University," *MIT Design Issues* 17 (2001): 3–14.

support the architectural projects with signage, symbols, and brochures. My first project was to work on an identity and signage program for Place Ville Marie in Montreal, Canada. I enjoyed working with architects and having substantial budgets for my projects. The collaboration with other professionals was energizing and exciting to me. During my second year with I.M. Pei, I received a phone call from Bud Leake, one of my schoolmates from Yale, who graduated in 1960. By this time, he was the president of the Maryland Institute College of Art in Baltimore. He wanted me to interview for a position teaching the foundation course and graphic design classes. Although I loved living in New York City, Tomás Maldonado's comments that I should consider a teaching career kept coming back to me. I decided that it was a challenge I couldn't pass up. So I interviewed, was hired, and jumped right into a full-time teaching schedule. KP: How did your expectations of teaching compare to the reality of being in front of a group of students and leading several different classes each day? PS: As with any new teacher, my first year was a bit shaky. Preparing for each class was incredibly time consuming. But during the second year I hit my stride and began to enjoy what I was doing.[9] I even added a photography class to my already hectic teaching schedule. At that same time, I met Patricia Umholtz, a lovely young lady who had just finished her degree in art education. We were married in the summer of 1963. In the midst of this wildly busy time, I received a phone call from Martin Friedman at the Walker Art Center saying that he was finally ready to hire a design director and curator. He wanted to interview me in Minneapolis. Since I once thought that working in a museum would be my dream job, it seemed obvious that I should check out this new opportunity. KP: What were your first impressions of the Twin Cities, in general, and the Walker Art Center, in particular? PS: Well, I flew to Minneapolis in March 1964. The weather was unusually mild that year, so it wasn't the frozen tundra I had expected. I had never been west of the Mississippi River before, so I felt like I was on a frontier of sorts, even though Minneapolis was a bustling city. Rob Roy Kelly, the director of the design department at the Minneapolis School of Art, showed me around and I liked the feel of the place, especially the lakes and park system. In my interview, I discovered the Walker job would allow me to work on a variety of design projects. My responsibilities would include designing and curating exhibitions, designing and editing catalogues and the *Design Quarterly* magazine, and designing posters for the new Guthrie Theater, which was attached to the Walker. It was three jobs rolled into one. A lot of work to be sure, but how could I resist such a plum job? KP: Moving to the Midwest was a big change. What made you think that this was the right personal and professional decision at this time? PS: Pat and I decided it was worth the risk to move to a new city for such an interesting job. Even at that time, the Walker Art Center had a reputation for being on the leading edge of contemporary art, and Martin was one of the few museum directors who also actively championed modern design. In fact, the Twin Cites was considered a cultural

9. Seitz's foundation course at the Maryland Institute College of Art, which combined elements of foundation classes he had taken at HfG Ulm and Yale, was very well received. Also of particular note was his color theory course, based on the one taught by Josef Albers at Yale.

oasis. Between here and Chicago, there was nothing. Between here and San Francisco, there was nothing. I thought that this was a place, the right place, for me to make a difference. So, after the second semester ended in Baltimore, we moved to Minneapolis. At age thirty-three, I was ready for another fresh start. My years at the Walker were a culmination of all the things I wanted to do in several design disciplines. It was a time of great professional growth for me. I had so many new responsibilities—designing exhibits from scratch, gathering visual images from all over the world, editing everything, creating educational programs, and working with the docents—that I often felt overwhelmed. Remember, in the mid-sixties, it was just me and an occasional assistant in the design department. We worked very hard, year in and year out. It was exhausting and exhilarating at the same time!   KP: Tell us about some of the specific projects you worked on at the Walker Art Center [pages 99 to 117]. PS: Where do I start? I am particularly proud of the topics in modern design and architecture we featured in the *Design Quarterlies* I edited, especially a double issue called *Design and the Computer* in 1966 [pages 104 and 105]. It was an issue that was way ahead of its time. I'm also pleased that we developed many interesting exhibitions [*Toward a New City, Furniture by Breuer/Le Corbusier/Mies van der Rohe 1924–1931*, and *Mass Transit: Problem and Promise*] that were among the first to introduce modern design to a Midwestern audience. When the Walker closed in 1969 for construction [of its new building] I knew that the design department would be in limbo for at least two years. I didn't know what I would do for those two years, so I began to think of other career options. I could have traveled in the United States and in Europe and gather materials for future design shows, but I thought that this would be a good time to start a design business of my own.   KP: Tell us about the transition from design director and curator at the Walker to becoming a design entrepreneur. PS: Walking away from the Walker was difficult, but I knew I had to try to make it on my own. Launching a new business is a big risk, especially when you have a family to support, but Pat and I decided it was what we needed to do. My first design firm was called Visual Communications. Because of my contacts with the Walker, I had several good clients right away. I continued designing posters and promotional materials for the Guthrie Theater [pages 118 and 119], and worked on printed materials for Hazelden Treatment Center, Carleton College, and the Minneapolis Public Library. I also did my first corporate identity program for Velie Motors in Brooklyn Park. But I missed the multidisciplinary collaboration that was such an important part of my work at the Walker, so I started to organize a design cooperative called the Community Design Center. It enabled local graphic designers and architects to collaborate and provide pro bono services for social causes in the metro area.   KP: Did your experience working at the Community Design Center influence your decision to start InterDesign? PS: Yes! That's when I started thinking about forming a group of designers and architects to do interdisciplinary design projects. After several meetings, architects Duane Thorbeck and Alfred

French, landscape architect Roger B. Martin, and I decided to launch InterDesign, the Twin Cites first interdisciplinary design firm. (Later, Stephen Kahne, a computer specialist from the University of Minnesota, joined our partnership.) Our collaborative philosophy and interdisciplinary approach were distinctly different from the way design was typically practiced in this area. In the early 1970s, the business community was familiar with the persuasive graphics of advertising, but did not understand the importance of information design and identity systems. InterDesign helped educate corporate leaders about the value of interdisciplinary design and introduced them to the idea that good design was good business. We started with a small urban-planning project for the town of New Ulm, Minnesota. But, thanks to a booming economy and a progressive business community, we had many forward-thinking clients and developed a reputation for creative collaboration and for developing strategic design systems. This led to a variety of groundbreaking projects [pages 123 to 147], including the identity programs and signage systems for the Minneapolis Parkways, the downtown St. Paul Skyways, the Minnesota State Capital, and the Minnesota Zoo. We lived to design.   KP: Can you believe that at this time there was no listing for "Graphic Design" in the Yellow Pages? PS: Well, in 1970, I made history of sorts by requesting that that specific category be included. That year InterDesign was the one and only graphic design firm listed.   KP: During this same time, you also began teaching at the Minneapolis College of Art and Design (MCAD). That must have been a challenge. Tell us what made you choose to add teaching to your already full professional practice. PS: It was a challenge! I thought it was important for practicing designers to work with aspiring young designers and help them to develop a variety of skills necessary in the real world of graphic design. I also felt it was important for me to give something back to the community. I had also been interested in computer graphics for quite some time, and wanted to assemble a state-of-the-art laboratory at MCAD.[10] I strongly believed that students needed to become familiar with and well versed in this new technology. I wanted to integrate the teaching of graphic design and computer graphics in such a way that design skills were not confused with or displaced by computer skills.   KP: Didn't you also become actively involved in SIGGRAPH during this period? PS: Yes. In the early 1980s, I met Dick Mueller, a vice president at Control Data, who introduced me to SIGGRAPH, a professional computer graphics organization. The acronym stands for Special Interest Group in Computer Graphics. Dick and I worked together for the SIGGRAPH Conference, which was held in Minneapolis in 1984. It was a major coup for a city this size to host such a big conference. In fact, the Herculean task of accommodating more than twenty thousand attendees helped the city of Minneapolis to move forward and build a larger, more accommodating convention center. This conference was one of several events that put the Twin Cities on the map as a center for progressive design.   KP: What about the founding of the Minnesota Graphic Designers Association (MGDA)? Weren't you also a part

10. In the early 1980s, the computer lab at MCAD was outfitted with several Apple computers and a new Macintosh for student use. It also included three dedicated computer systems for specific design tasks—a Dicomed D38, a Florida Computer Graphics system, and a 3M BFA Paint system.

of those early organizational efforts? PS: Oh, yes. In the 1970s, besides the Art Directors Club, there was no professional design organization in the Twin Cites to represent graphic design. We definitely wanted to define graphic design as different from commercial art, the term that had been used up until then. It was frustrating because we always had to explain what graphic design was and why it was an important strategic tool for businesses. The State of Minnesota decided to create a new license plate in 1976. My colleague, Tim Larsen, thought they should hire a professional designer. He and Kevin Kuester went to the Legislative Committee meeting to voice their opinion, which was basically ignored. The only comments that were taken seriously were those of the Minnesota License Plate Collectors Club. Afterward, in frustration, Tim asked their representative how many members were in their club. His answer? Five. That's when Tim realized that if graphic designers were to have any say in the public arena, they would need to be a part of a professional organization. It was our goal to "raise the bar" for quality design. We were creating a new identity for this new profession. Thanks to Tim's tireless leadership, our small community of graphic designers slogged through all of the tedious tasks necessary to form a nonprofit professional organization. MGDA became "official" in 1977.[11] I was elected president for the term 1978 to 1979.   KP: You certainly had a lot going on concurrently, how did you handle this incredibly demanding schedule? PS: My strong work ethic and organizational skills were quite useful, but I have to say that the overwhelming demands of my daily schedule took a toll on both my personal and professional life. At InterDesign, the commitment to the interdisciplinary approach to design projects waned. So after ten years, I left the company. Over the course of the next two years, I worked with Hideki Yamamoto and Miranda Moss (formerly Pat Seitz) to form a new company called Seitz Yamamoto Moss. Our new design firm focused on corporate identity projects and packaging design, and our clients included 3M, Control Data, Lutheran Brotherhood, Minnesota Life Insurance, Miracle Ear, and many other Fortune 500 companies. I also started to get involved in naming projects and what we now call "brand identity" and "strategic design." The Fargo Hospital and Clinic, which became MeritCare, was a good example.   KP: You founded one more design firm before you retired. Tell us about that. PS: In the mid-1980s, my first marriage broke up and I left Seitz Yamamoto Moss. Once again, I had to start over. I called my new design firm Peter Seitz & Associates. I was particularly interested in pursuing systems design, and did some interesting work for Ecolab and 3M. Then I was asked to do the identity and signage system for the new Convention Center in Minneapolis. My new design firm also did design projects for the Mayo Clinic in Rochester, Minnesota. In 1988, I teamed up with John Lees, my classmate from Yale, and we designed the identity and signage system for the Pacifico Convention and Exhibition Center in Yokohama, Japan [page 150]. In the late 1980s, thanks in part to the national prominence of the Fallon McElligot & Rice advertising agency and Duffy Design,

11. Later MGDA elected to affiliate with the national American Institute of Graphic Arts (AIGA) organization, becoming AIGA Minnesota in 1986.

the Twin Cities was seen as "hot" advertising and design market. Minnesota became an attractive location for many new designers and small design firms. Supported by the amazing new computer technology that streamlined the design and production processes, the design market became quite competitive. I realized it was time for me to refocus, concentrate more on teaching, and prepare for retirement. KP: How did you prepare for retirement? Did you know what you wanted to do for the rest of your life? PS: Moving to the country had been in the back of my mind for quite awhile. After all of those relentlessly hectic years of work and raising a family, I wanted a quieter and more peaceful way of life. I started looking for property south of the Twin Cities, but I couldn't find anything I liked that was in my price range. So, I started looking at land in Wisconsin. To get the site and acreage I dreamed of, I had to go all the way down to Pepin, which is ninety miles from Minneapolis. I found a beautiful piece of land just outside of town. After the plot was purchased, I designed a floor plan, and took the sketches I had been working on to my friend and former colleague Bob Lambert. He did the architectural drawings and the construction process began. To make a long story short, after an extended period of steel construction (which was unusual for residential housing), I moved into my new house one year later in 1996 [page 173]. Much of the interior work had not been completed because I hoped to save money by doing it myself. I'm still working on it! KP: But you were still teaching at MCAD, so you really didn't retire yet, did you? PS: Well, even with the long commute, I did continue to teach at MCAD one day a week, and even agreed to be interim chair of the design department after Kristen McDougall resigned in 1998. After that I was asked to teach part of a graduate critique course in the MFA program. So, you are correct, I really didn't retire until 2002. However, all the while I was getting acquainted with people in my new community. I became actively involved in the local Lutheran church and got to know other artistically inclined people living nearby. I started watercolor painting, and before I knew it, I was on a committee to open an art and design center in Pepin. That has been my latest labor of love. KP: Based on your life experiences, what advice or words of wisdom do you have for young designers today? PS: Design your life! As I said before, actively make your own decisions rather than having them passively made for you. It is important to set goals, in writing, and review them periodically. In today's fast-paced, ever-changing global economy, and I know this sounds archaic, but make a one-year plan, and then make a five-year plan. Decide what you need to aim at for the next twelve months. Be flexible, but always reach beyond what you think is achievable. Stay open to change, work for change, and do your best to make it happen.

PLANNING OPERATIONS

DESIGN
FUNCTION

MGMT.
FUNCTION

InterDesign

left to right: Duane Thorbeck, Alfred French, Stephen Kahne, Peter Seitz, and Roger B. Martin at InterDesign, circa 1970

The Art of Collaboration:
The Design Practices of Peter Seitz

Bruce N. Wright, AIA
Editor, *Fabric Architecture* magazine

Design Partnerships

"Can you draw a rock?" These words were my first introduction to Peter Seitz, a founding partner in the interdisciplinary collaborative design studio called InterDesign, Inc., as he previewed my qualifications by phone for a position at the firm. It was June 1974, and InterDesign was the lead studio for a proposed new Minnesota Zoo. Seitz was looking for someone to assist in the design and detailing of artificial rockwork for all the animal exhibits in this multi-million dollar state-funded project. "I need someone who can draw rocks, can you do that?" After the briefest of pauses, my answer was, "Certainly!"

I had no idea why I would need to draw rocks, but if being able to draw rocks meant getting a job at the most coveted design firm in town, then I was determined to prove I was up to the challenge. When I presented my design portfolio in person to Seitz a week or so later, it included some magazine layouts I had done from my years at the University of Minnesota, a few student architecture projects I thought might impress him, such as a street furniture system I had designed for one of my architecture professors named Duane "Dewey" Thorbeck (whom I knew to be a partner at InterDesign), and of course several sketches of rock outcroppings. He complimented me on my rock drawings, but expressed some skepticism about my usefulness to his department because I was not trained as a graphic designer, and excusing me, said he would let me know about the position. I left somewhat discouraged, but a few days later he called to say that

Entrance of InterDesign Inc., circa 1970

I got the job and was to start immediately![1] My life was changed forever. This was the summer of the Watergate trials, the publishing of Woodward and Bernstein's *All the President's Men*, Richard M. Nixon's resignation as President of the United States, and InterDesign's fifth straight year working on the zoo.

InterDesign grew out of the social activism of the 1960s and early 1970s, a time when designers were encouraged to engage in community causes and many believed in design's ability to solve all of society's problems. This optimism was a carry-over from the European influence of the Bauhaus on American design schools by its ex-patriots, such as Walter Gropius at Harvard and Josef Albers and Herbert Matter at Yale, where Seitz and Thorbeck studied. The late 1960s witnessed a growing recognition by architects and designers of the complexity of design problems and from this a realization that collaborative design teams were needed to tackle these difficult projects. The Architects' Collaborative (TAC)—started by Gropius in 1945 in Cambridge, Massachusetts—was a national role model of team practice. InterDesign partners Thorbeck and Roger B. Martin, the landscape architect on the team who had studied at the Harvard Graduate School of Design (GSD) in the early 1960s, acknowledge Gropius' and TAC's influences on the shaping of their design thinking.[2]

But world events also informed the partners' thinking, as Thorbeck acknowledged. "Peter and I started a discussion [in 1968 or early 1969] about creating an interdisciplinary design firm." He notes two worldwide developments that influenced designers: "One, we were getting our first images of the planet Earth back from outer space.[3] You know, there was a very strong environmental, ecological bent [to design thinking]. Secondly, the feeling was that design problems were of a nature that one discipline alone could not address them; that it really required a very strong interdisciplinary approach. And it was these ideas of interdisciplinary design that inspired our concept of InterDesign."[4]

However, a unique aspect of InterDesign was Seitz's leadership as an equal partner alongside architects Thorbeck and Alfred "Al" W. French III (another of the founding partners), and landscape architect Martin. This was unprecedented on the national design scene, and preceded by three years the British design firm Pentagram, a design consultancy with which InterDesign is most often compared. InterDesign opened its doors in 1969; the London-based Pentagram—a five-way partnership between graphic designers Alan Fletcher, Colin Forbes, and Mervyn Kurlansky, architect Theo Crosby and product designer Kenneth Grange—was formed in 1972.

What gave Seitz the courage and confidence to stand as an equal at the creation of a new breed of design firm? Perhaps a look at his years as design curator and editor at the Walker Art Center will shed some light on this question.

1. I later learned that Peter Seitz had discussed my work with Duane Thorbeck and expressed his hesitation about hiring me, to which Thorbeck replied, "Oh, I know Bruce [from my studio at the school of architecture]—he's good. Hire him!" **2.** Personal interviews with Duane Thorbeck, FAIA (August 12, 2005) and Roger B. Martin, FASLA (August 14, 2007). **3.** The December 1968 moon orbit of Apollo 8 produced the first Earthrise photographs, regarded by some to have sparked the environmental movement. **4.** Interview with Thorbeck, August 12, 2005.

Duane Thorbeck leads a site-planning presentation for the University
of Minnesota project, circa 1970

When Seitz was hired as the museum's new designer and design curator at age thirty-three by Walker Art Center director Martin Friedman in June of 1964, the Beatles had just made their first visit to the United States and the Civil Rights Act was passed. Only a year earlier John F. Kennedy had been assassinated; in Minneapolis, the Guthrie Theater had opened its first season with the repertory plays of *Hamlet*, *The Miser*, *The Three Sisters*, and *Death of a Salesman*. It was a troubled time of civil unrest and social upheaval, but the country remained optimistic about its future; likewise, many designers felt strongly about their ability to make positive changes in society.

The Walker Art Center, which had garnered national and international respect as a forward-thinking cultural institution, could trace its modernist design roots to its founding as a public art center in 1940. The Walker's *Design Quarterly* regularly published reviews of internationally acclaimed modern designers, and it had originated several important design exhibitions that traveled the country in the 1940s and early 1950s. With Seitz's arrival, the Walker would take a significant leap forward in cementing its reputation of advanced thinking and influence. With his European education (Hochschule für Gestaltung Ulm, Germany 1955 to 1959) and East Coast graduate school connections (Yale, 1959 to 1961), he brought together important thinkers from around the world for conferences and exhibitions, and, as editor of *Design Quarterly* (*DQ*), published landmark treatises on design, such as *Signs and Symbols in Graphic Communication* (*DQ* 62, 1965), Rudolph Arnheim's *Dynamics of Shape* (*DQ* 64, 1966), *Mass Transit: Problems and Promise* (*DQ* 71, 1968) and the seminal double issue *Design and the Computer* (*DQ* 66/67, 1967). "His solid understanding of modernism and his international point of view were important to me," says Friedman. "He had a lot of international contacts who were valuable to the exhibitions we mounted. I liked the way he looked in all directions. He brought a holistic view to design."[5]

Many of these international contacts were architects, so Seitz was comfortable conversing with them, speaking their professional language. In fact, his exceptional ability to visualize design concepts coming from all fields was sought after by many architects because he could express graphically what others might only verbalize. Of the eleven Walker exhibitions designed and/or curated by Seitz, three were about architecture; and four of the ten issues of *Design Quarterly* edited by him focused on architecture or urban design.

To Seitz, graphic design was part of a larger notion of communicating ideas, a tool like other design tools that could be put into service toward a common goal, a social good. Not only was graphic design (a term, incidentally, that only came into widespread usage in the 1970s) part of his bag of tricks, but so were any and all visual methods that could be exploited to further a project. He called this "visual communications" rather

5. Phone interview with Martin Friedman, August 25, 2004.

Exhibition design for *Furniture by Breuer/Le Corbusier/Mies van der Rohe 1924–1931* at the Walker Art Center, 1966

than graphic design, in deference to his training at HfG Ulm, where degrees were granted in visual communications. "Peter never thought of himself as a graphic designer," says Thorbeck. "He always called himself a visual communicator, which included signs and signage, corporate reports, logos, and all of the things normally included under the typographic arts, but he also was into environmental graphics and environmental design, exhibit design, and interior design."[6] "Peter was a delight to work with as a part of the interdisciplinary effort [at InterDesign]," says Roger Martin. "The thing that I really appreciated about him was he could take an idea and clearly visualize it. He really helped the Zoo Board [the governing body on the Minnesota Zoological Gardens project] understand and see clearly what our ideas were. This visualization helped sell us when getting work. That, I think, gave us an advantage" over other design firms.

Given all of this, and the fact that prior to joining the Walker Seitz worked briefly in the graphic design studios of New York architect I.M. Pei,[7] a strong case can be made that he was not intimidated by architects, but viewed them as partners in designing a better social life. As he says of his term with I.M. Pei, "I enjoyed working with architects and working with the design professionals. . . . You had real budgets: four-color process and dye cuts, and square formats, full-sized formats. To go after a building project that might cost $200 million, they would send out a $10,000 brochure—at that time a princely amount!"[8]

New Tools, New Ideas

An exhibition on mass transit problems, an issue of *Design Quarterly* on the use of computers in design—these are contemporary concerns, are they not? The surprise is that Seitz was addressing these topics with serious research and substantive answers forty years ago, and, in the case of design's use of the computer, before the invention of the Apple Macintosh or any other personal computer. Yet, all of these ideas were grist for his intellectual mill, weighty enough for him to recognize their importance to all designers, to incorporate them into his own practice and to share them with his colleagues and protégées. These were not idle curiosities for Seitz, but serious scholarly pursuits that warranted deep analysis and the brightest minds available. With his links to European design communities and contacts from Yale, he was able to engage the top thinkers on any subject and get them to write about it for *Design Quarterly* or for an exhibition. This predilection for bringing diverse thinkers together to create new responses to questions or design challenges served him well throughout his professional career, particularly in helping to establish InterDesign and in his teaching at the Minneapolis College of Art and Design (MCAD). A design exhibition is the result of collaboration between curator and artist, exhibition subject, or source—a team effort—and interpreting a subject for public consumption is the essence of Seitz's training as a visual communicator; teaching is also a collaboration between teacher and student.

6. Interview with Thorbeck, August 12, 2005.   7. The design studio at I.M. Pei and Associates, New York, was one of the first such in-house graphic design studios within an architectural office in the United States. Seitz worked on several projects for Pei after graduating from Yale in 1961, designing signage, reports, and other collateral that supported the architectural work. One major project in the studio at the time was the signage and identity for the Place Ville-Marie buildings and plaza by I.M. Pei in Montreal, Canada. A partner in the graphics studio at the time was Ken Resen, also a Yale alumnus. "Peter was wonderful" in the studio, says Resen. He remembers Seitz well and liked his work ethic. Phone interview with Ken Resen, August 24, 2007.   8. Interview with Peter Seitz, November 8, 2002.

Exhibition design for *Mass Transit: Problem and Promise* at the
Walker Art Center, 1968

Digital typesetting system at the offices of
Seitz Graphic Directions, circa 1978

It is inevitable that working with such leading thinkers as Martin Krampen, a schoolmate of Seitz's at HfG Ulm, would impress him with revolutionary concepts such as using computers to control design elements or shape line and form. In 1966 Krampen invited him to attend an international conference on computers in design and communication held in Waterloo, Canada. What he learned at that conference excited and inspired him to edit a book on the subject with Krampen.[9] From this point on, Seitz was an early advocate for the use of computer technology by designers. He wrote many articles for design journals about why computers should not be feared but embraced as another tool for expression.[10]

While at the Walker, Seitz also met Stephen Kahne, an associate professor of electrical engineering at the University of Minnesota and director of the university's hybrid computer lab. Their common interest in the computer as a new tool for design led to their later collaboration at InterDesign. Kahne's specialty was systems analysis and advanced computer design and programming, and he brought this skill and access to the University of Minnesota's mainframe computer to the firm when it formed in the late 1960s, an advantage over other design firms: first, when InterDesign went after the original competition for the Minnesota Zoological Gardens project, and second, after winning the commission, applying the computer's capacity to analyze large numbers of variables and huge amounts of data collected about four potential sites for the zoo to help select the final site. Landscape architect Martin felt certain the use of computers helped InterDesign on numerous occasions in overcoming competition from rival design firms, especially when it came to the zoo, a highly desirable project for any firm at the time. The use of computers in design "was very rare for the time. Unusual!" says Martin. "The computers were used to analyze the zoo sites in a systematical way and helped justify clearly with documentation what the options for the sites were. I think that helped convince our clients beyond a doubt."[11] But Seitz foresaw myriad opportunities to utilize the computer throughout his practice. He applied it to identity systems, including logo designs. Eventually, all graphic designers would catch up with this embrace of the computer as an essential tool.

The Walker provided other connections that continued to echo throughout Seitz's career and the local design community. By the mid-1960s when he arrived in the Twin Cities, a group of dedicated modernists had gathered through the Walker to form the Center Design Council. An elite coterie of business leaders and some of the top as well as up-and-coming designers from the region, the Center Design Council included the likes of Ralph Rapson, Robert Cerny, Alfred French, and a young Duane Thorbeck, the board's president. Although Seitz had heard about Thorbeck while at Yale, the two did not formally meet until Seitz came to the Walker.[12] Perhaps because of their shared graduate school experience, or because they both had strong interest in all aspects of design, they hit it off instantly. Seitz

9. Martin Krampen and Peter Seitz, eds., *Design and Planning 2: Computers in Design and Communications* (New York: Hastings House, 1967). A subsequent double issue of *Design Quarterly* addressed the same topic: *Design Quarterly 66/67: Design and the Computer* (1967). 10. For more on Seitz's establishment of a computer graphics program at MCAD, see page 68 in this volume. 11. Interview with Roger B. Martin, August 14, 2007. 12. Thorbeck describes his time at Yale while Seitz was there: "I didn't know him well, but because the graphic design and the architecture departments were not working together but were in the same building—they [graphics] were down on the lowest level and we were on the top level—I do recall briefly seeing him in passing." Interview with Thorbeck, August 12, 2005.

Peter Seitz and Duane Thorbeck, president of the Center
Design Council, at the Walker Art Center, circa 1966

encouraged Thorbeck to exhibit some of his students' work from the University at the Walker, and Thorbeck enthusiastically supported Seitz's wide-ranging interests in and exhibitions on such subjects as urban design, graphic symbols, transportation issues, and international designers.

Thorbeck recalls Seitz's broad interest in all design, especially when he was part of InterDesign: "I'd say, that of anyone in the group, Peter was the one that reached out across very broad areas of interest. From interior design to product design to—and I do believe that Peter designed some furniture—to graphic design," he was interested in it all.[13]

New Businesses, New Directions

Just as Seitz enthusiastically conquered the museum world, his approach to the business world was equally passionate and transformative. We've seen how key contacts made while at the Walker led him to the discovery and adoption of new tools for design, and how new friendships led to future partnerships and clients, to the gradual building of a network of trusted design talent that he called upon for numerous projects. His extensive professional network speaks to his generosity of inclusion, his spirit of collaboration embodied by the teams he put together over the years.

In 1967, during a period of social unrest across the country, Seitz found himself conflicted as well. The Walker Art Center was about to begin its first major restructuring with a proposed new building designed by Edward Larrabee Barnes. This meant that all museum staff would be dislocated and dispersed between several rented spaces in downtown Minneapolis while the old building was demolished and the new one built—at least a two-year process. In a sense, the museum would shut down for two years and Seitz was uncertain whether this arrangement made sense for his future as a designer, prompting him to consider possible alternatives. "I didn't quite know what I would do for two years and I thought [that I was] too busy to sit around for two years doing nothing, waiting until they built it."[14] With a staff of one, and too much to do, he felt his own design work was being subsumed by the larger demands of the museum's shows. Of this period he recalls thinking, "If I work here another five years, I would have ten years of work in design in whatever sculpture and whatever mannerist painter or whatever style [was shown in the main galleries]. My own design will be overlooked, will be lost within the work of the museum." It was time for him to venture out on his own. The act of leaving the Walker led him to start the first of several influential design firms in Twin Cities. Before his departure, however, he demanded help with the tremendous workload. "I did three jobs by myself," he says. "A year before I left, I told Martin I needed help, that I couldn't do it [by myself] because I normally was working ten to twelve hour days. Four times a week I went back at night" to work on projects.[15] Friedman hired an assistant for Seitz who proved to be quite capable at the diverse design demands

13. Ibid.   14. Interview with Seitz, November 8, 2002. 15. Ibid.

of a dynamic art museum. Gay Beste (now Beste Reineck), a recent graduate of the Royal College of Art, London, arrived in June of that year, quickly taking on the full gamut of design responsibilities.[16]

"I had heard that Peter wanted a European-trained graphic designer," says Reineck. "They [the Walker] had placed an advertisement in *Graphis* magazine; three or four lines requesting a graphic designer and that the hire would be working for a contemporary art museum. I was working at the time in a London design office as an assistant to a designer. I'm not sure why I wrote an answer to the ad, but I did. And I'd completely forgotten about it when I got a telegram from the director [Friedman], who said he would be in town staying at a certain hotel and would be holding interviews. We met and I presented my portfolio, and I remember thinking when I left the interview that somehow I knew I had the job, that I felt I needed that job. And then the director said that he would hire me. It took eight months to get a work permit and all the paperwork cleared."[17] Reineck started at the Walker in June 1967, working for Seitz. "I [had] heard all kinds of stories that he was difficult to work for, strict and a German, but it was absolutely wonderful. We had a wonderful working relationship. He explained a lot, and he left me to do a lot on my own. I imagine he was busy organizing the exhibitions and editing *DQ*, etc. I basically focused on all the publications that came out of the office (relating to exhibitions). Of course, we designed the shows too. I had some incredible experiences working on design [at the Walker]."

In spite of the extra help he got from his first and only assistant, and with the imminent shut down of the Walker looming ahead, Seitz felt the urge to move on. "I'd been there about two years when I learned that Peter was planning on leaving [to go off and start his own firm]," says Reineck. "And he left me there to work alone."

The Power of Visual Communication

The name of Seitz's first wholly independent design firm reflected his belief in the power of graphic design as a business tool. With several freelance design jobs in hand and many good connections garnered from the Walker, he launched Visual Communications, Inc. (VCI) in 1968, and attempted to place a listing in the local business directory. Clients included the Guthrie Theater (which was already a freelance client during his tenure at the Walker and continues as his first job under the new name), Hazelden Treatment Centers, the Minneapolis Public Library, and Carleton College. During this period Seitz also organized the Community Design Center (CDC), a design cooperative that enabled local graphic designers and architects to collaborate and provide pro bono work for social causes in the Twin Cities area. The CDC first locates at 118 East 26th Street, Minneapolis, just a block from the Minneapolis College of Art and Design.[18] VCI operated for approximately two years when Seitz hatched a new collaborative design firm, InterDesign, with friends Thorbeck, French, Kahne, and Martin.

16. Interview with Gay Beste Reineck, August 18, 2007. 17. Ibid.   18. See pages 56 to 58 in this volume.

Peter Seitz in the design studio at the Walker Art Center, circa 1965

top: InterDesign colleagues (left to right): Duane Thorbeck, Roger B. Martin, Robert Lambert, and Peter Seitz, 1983   **bottom:** Design critique at InterDesign, circa 1970

To claim that InterDesign was the single most influential design firm to come out of the Twin Cities during the mid-century decades would be only the slightest of exaggerations. From the start, the firm captured attention and respect from designers and clients with its unorthodox approach to solving design problems.[19] Seitz's unique perspective on design and visual expression, including his belief and embrace of technology as a tool, helped launch InterDesign with flair and brilliance.

The biggest coup for the young firm came within weeks of opening its doors. The announcement of an open competition for the design of a new zoo for Minnesota had all the elements of interdisciplinary practice that InterDesign was created to serve. "We thought that here was a project that we were just made for," recalls Thorbeck. "It involved exhibits, a lot of signage. . . environmental graphics and environmental design, and exhibit design, interior design" as well as architecture, landscape design, and site analysis.[20]

InterDesign entered and won the competition, then quickly hired staff to take on the workload, establishing three primary "studios" under the three main disciplines of architecture, landscape architecture, and graphic design. Many former associates were tapped by the partners; Seitz called on Gay Beste Reineck as one of his first hires. "Shortly after [leaving the Walker] Peter called me to come work at his new firm InterDesign. And Martin [Friedman] told me: 'Don't do it! It will be the biggest mistake of your career.' But I knew I needed to work with Peter, and I did and I had a wonderful time. We did a lot of good design [at InterDesign]."[21]

Many talented designers worked in the office when it was in full force. There are estimates that InterDesign spawned more than fifteen spin-off design firms from all of the talent that passed through the office in its fifteen years of operation. Some of those known to have begun and maintained independent graphic design practices include Reineck (Reineck and Reineck Design), Sandy Stein (Stein, LLC), Herman Reller, Kevin Kuester (the Kuester Group), Kerry Peterson (later a photographer with Marvy! Advertising Photography), and Patrick Redmond. Hideki Yamamoto, a senior designer at InterDesign in the 1970s, became a partner in the Peter Seitz studio that was the first to break away from InterDesign in 1980. From the landscape architecture studio of InterDesign, several people started their own professional firms, including Damon Farber (Damon Farber & Assoc.), Bryan Carlson, and Harold Skjelbostad. Architects who left the office to form independent firms include John Weidt (the Weidt Group), Chuck Kubat (Kubat Consulting), Terry Wobken, and Steve McNeil.

A short list of people who passed though the office and went on to successful careers in design or design-related activities includes: Jim Dustrude (principal transportation

19. Robert Jensen, "Urban Revitalization of New Ulm, Minnesota by InterDesign Inc., Minneapolis," *Architectural Record* (December 1972): 92; part of the series "Young Architects on Their Own." 20. Interview with Thorbeck, August 12, 2005. 21. Interview with Reineck, August 18, 2007.

strategist, Minnesota Department of Transportation Office of Transit and Bikes); Cindy Fern Lamb (Lamb Art Direction); Craig Hess (partner in an architectural firm); Chuck Koosmann (an independent photographer); Neal Libson (director of a real estate management firm); and Cotty Lowry (successful real estate agent in Twin Cities). My own affiliation with InterDesign, from (1974 to 1976), also influenced my career as editor of an international architecture journal.

At some point in the life cycle of InterDesign, challenging graphic design opportunities were not coming at the rate previously enjoyed at its beginning. Graphic design problems, although important to the firm's overall functioning, settled into being routine cover designs for project brochures, bid packages, and land analysis reports—hardly inspiring for a studio filled with top graphic talent.[22] Seitz realized it meant more of what he had done years ago while at I.M. Pei and Associates—graphic covers to sell the architecture (or in this case, both the architecture and landscape architecture) services. It was time again to split and start anew.

With an amicable departure, he took the graphic design studio en masse to start Seitz Graphic Directions, which specialized in corporate identity design, corporate mark (logo) design, and related design services. The firm occupied the first floor of his East Lake Harriet home.[23] Again, with good client connections, Seitz Graphic Directions had a strong start with clients such as Lutheran Brotherhood (now Thrivent Financial for Lutherans); Control Data Corporation; Miracle Ear; American Medical Systems; the State of Minnesota; Hammel, Green and Abrahamson (HGA); Gelco Corporation; and Ellerbe Associates. As its office brochure from the period describes: "We strip a company down to its essence, look at the mission statement and how they describe themselves. Then we try to extract key words and attributes, construct words with root reference to what they do and translate them into marketing-oriented phrasing."

The studio was one of only two or three design firms in the Twin Cities "at the time doing anything of this nature," says Miranda Moss. "This was sort of the beginning of this type of corporate graphic design in Minneapolis. We had the Minneapolis Park Board—doing all the signage and wayfinding—because InterDesign had initially worked on it."[24]

After two years, the firm's name changed to Seitz Yamamoto Moss to acknowledge its three principals—Seitz, Hideki Yamamoto, and Miranda Moss.[25] The studio further specialized in corporate identity projects and packaging design.

Businesses can become all consuming, if one lets them. Some people throw themselves into work as a way to avoid problems, others as a self-fulfilling outlet for abundant energy. Perhaps both could be true for Seitz. After a few years of full-bore design work and management of Seitz Yamamoto Moss (SYM), he found

22. Interview with Seitz, November 8, 2002.   23. Interview with Miranda Moss (formerly Pat Seitz), October 11, 2007. "It was Peter's idea to start the new company, and so he and Hideki formed a business to do more corporate design work. Peter wanted to do that type of work, rather than just teach it. I had my own business doing illustrations (Bjorkland's, for example), research, and design for InterDesign and corporate designs for clients. They decided to join me and set up the business in the house."   24. Ibid   25. Ibid "When we realized that we wanted to grow the business, the name needed to change," says Moss. "If I was to be treated as more than just the boss's wife, as an equal design partner, then I needed to change my name. I took the name of my daughter [Miranda] and the maiden name of my mother [Moss] and combined them. At first I thought it would be just a business name, and that I'd keep my name [Pat Seitz], but it became problematic to have two names, so it became my legal name."

The principals of Seitz Yamamoto Moss (left to right): Peter Seitz,
Miranda Moss, and Hideki Yamamoto, circa 1982

himself starting another design firm. This time, the name would involve no business partners, but simply himself—Peter Seitz & Associates—to reflect a more streamlined approach, and to indicate to potential clients that they were getting the master designer himself.

"What I wanted to do was create a company that wasn't just doing the typical kind of work. I wanted to make use of the skills I had, and still work with the interdisciplinary idea, the 'systems idea' that you do things which connect to other things. So I would design not just a brochure, but a brochure which also has to be packaged, or a product which has to be packaged, or a product which has to be *named.* Which all meant that you know these things, that you can solve these problems, and you can make a good income from it: doing things which not everybody does."[26]

Work for the new firm included a corporate identity manual for Ecolab, signage for the Minneapolis Convention Center, Edina's Centennial Lakes retail area, the Mayo Clinic, the Pacifico Convention and Exhibition Center in Yokohama, Japan, and packaging design for 3M and other clients. "Because I didn't have any partners, it was a very good time. And I had fun; I had good people, good projects. We had a nice location down at the Butler North building [in Minneapolis' Warehouse District], so we worked for four or five years in that building."[27] But the economy was changing in the late 1980s and Seitz found the need, like many businesses, to streamline. He moved his office into his home in Golden Valley and cut back to just himself and a secretary from 1991 to late 1995, when he closed his shop for good, while he continued to teach at MCAD.

Echoes within the Design and Business Communities—A Legacy

Although Seitz's influence was certainly significant with his colleagues, throughout all of his professional positions, it carries beyond the narrow design community to embrace the larger business and cultural communities of the state of Minnesota. His designs have affected many corporate and government organizations through visual impact studies for NSP, Northern States Power Co. (now Xcel Energy) and the Upper Mississippi River Wildlife and Fish Refuge as well as other major studies such as the Mississippi River Headwaters Reservoir Master Plan. His graphics made sense of InterDesign's campus master planning for IBM in Rochester, Minnesota, and his corporate identities for Lutheran Brotherhood, the Minneapolis Public Library, the Minnesota Zoo, Minnesota Mutual, and Gelco Corporation explained complex ideas in easily understood symbols and imagery. All of these non-design communities have benefited from his lucid vision and ability to communicate.

Today others who are working in the larger Twin Cities cultural community are following the high standards set by Seitz and his collaborators. The Walker has maintained its international status; the Twin Cities regularly win national design awards

26. Interview with Seitz, March 14, 2003. 27. Ibid.

for high-level designs in landscape, architecture, and graphic design. *Print* magazine often leads the Midwest section of its design annual with Minnesota, citing it as the bellwether of design in the Midwest. Although all of this cannot be attributed solely to Seitz, inarguably his influence has been felt throughout the Minnesota design and business communities and nationally within the graphic design world. The Twin Cities' design culture would not be what it is today were it not for Seitz's gentle and nurturing, yet insistent, guidance and leadership.

His life and work embodies the sense of promise engendered by modernism's utopian outlook, yet his ideals are leavened by the pragmatism of social responsibility and his Midwestern experiences. Several key individuals in his life—Max Bill, Otl Aicher, Josef Albers, Martin Friedman, and Martin Krampen— saw potential in him, encouraged and inspired him to become not only a good designer but also a designer with a social conscience. Seitz embodied these mentors' ideals and inspired others to carry them forward within their own lives.

Of her time working with Seitz at InterDesign and the Walker, Reineck reflects: "It was one of the best experiences of my life. We were talking once about the process, the design process. And he said, 'Well, you know Gay, you can apply it to anything, even your life.' I will always remember that. I learned a lot from Peter: how to organize things, how to design things, how to design a life!"[28]

28. Interview with Reineck, August 18, 2007.

Peter Seitz critiquing student design work at the Minneapolis College of Art and Design, 1986

Peter Seitz: A Catalyst for Creating Communities

Kolean Pitner, design historian and faculty member, College of Visual Arts, St. Paul

"To design is much more than simply to assemble, to order or even to edit: it is to add value and meaning, to illuminate, to simplify, to clarify, to modify, to dignify, to dramatize, to persuade, and perhaps even to amuse. To design is to transform prose into poetry." —Paul Rand

For more than fifty years, Minnesota has been a leader in artistic and design innovation. In his book *The Rise of the Creative Class*, Richard Florida reports, "the Twin Cites of Minneapolis and St. Paul have the seventh highest creativity index scores in the country."[1] Florida defines a creative community as a place "that is open to new people and ideas, where people network easily, and offbeat ideas are not stifled but turned into new projects, companies, and economic growth."[2] How did this happen? Why did it happen here?

Minnesota's famed "quality of life" has attracted well-educated and talented people like Peter Seitz from around the world. In turn, Seitz dedicated his career to shaping and improving our visual environment by bringing together the business, arts, and education communities in service to the common good. He helped make "the good life" in Minnesota even better. Believing that creativity and community go hand in hand, he has created communities at each step in his career through partnerships, collaborations, and cooperation. The Twin Cities design and education communities would not be blessed with so many top-notch graphic design firms if it weren't for Seitz's

[1]. Richard Florida, *The Rise of the Creative Class* (New York: Basic Books, 2002), Table 3. The Creativity Index Rank is based on three component scores—technology, talent, and tolerance—for forty-nine regions with a population of more than one million.   [2]. Ibid.

enormous influence on his former students and other local designers who have benefited both from his professional contributions and his dedication to quality design education. And the state's business community would not have flourished to the extent it has without his tireless advocacy for good design as a strategic business tool.

Marvelous Minnesota

Seitz was in the right place at the right time when he arrived in Minneapolis in 1964 for his new job as design curator at the Walker Art Center, one of the few museums in the country to champion modern art and design. Landing in the midst of a progressive political and cultural community with a booming economy, he had the good fortune to be among business and arts leaders with the resources and foresight to fund many of his inventive interdisciplinary design projects[3] and put into practice the maxim that "good design is good business." Thus, he was able to sow the seeds of modernist aesthetics and ideals into the culturally rich Minnesota landscape. "When I first came to Minneapolis, I was pleasantly surprised by the depth of the cultural life here. The Walker Art Center, the Minneapolis Institute of Arts, the Guthrie Theater, and the Minnesota Orchestra were all outstanding," says Seitz. "Plus there were the beautiful lakes and the parkway system. It felt like a promising place to begin the next phase of my career."[4]

Almost thirty-five years ago, in August 1973, *Time* magazine's cover featured a photo of Minnesota Governor Wendell Anderson, smiling broadly as he proudly held up a northern pike, with the headline "The Good Life in Minnesota." The accompanying article, "Minnesota: A State That Works," gave several clues as to why the Twin Cities was poised to develop a dynamic creative class, which became an important source for economic growth.[5] Looking back at that article, we see a picture of Minnesota at its finest, offering praises for the state's abundant natural resources, its hard-working people, its clean government, and its charitable spirit—even our infamously cold winter weather gets a positive spin. It was argued that Minnesota winters account for the social solidarity of the state: "You have to be strong and productive to survive here." A transplanted Chicagoan agreed, "Our winters build character and are a great blessing to us. You don't get the weak-kneed beach boys here." And all these kudos were before anyone knew anything about Lake Wobegon.

"By a combination of political and cultural tradition, geography and sheer luck, Minnesota nurtures an extraordinarily successful society." The article goes on to portray the state's economy as a well-balanced mix of manufacturing, agriculture, and services. Some of the nation's fastest-growing computer companies such as Honeywell, Control Data, and Univac were highlighted, along with 3M, General Mills, Pillsbury, and Investors Diversified Services (IDS). The glowing economic review continues: "Over the past ten years, Minnesota has become one of the nation's leading 'brain-industry' centers—more than 170 electronic and related

3. The Minnesota Zoo is an example of Seitz's visionary interdisciplinary design practice— a collaboration between various design disciplines, including architecture, graphic design, industrial design, landscape design, and city planning, to create large-scale projects both functional and beautiful. 4. Interview with Peter Seitz, November 8, 2002. 5. Quotations in this and the following five paragraphs are excerpted from Lance Marrow, "Minnesota: A State That Works," *Time* 13, August 13, 1973: 24–35

technical businesses now employ more than 70,000 people."

If there is a secret to Minnesota's success in creating the good life, the article suggests that it lies in people's extraordinary civic interest, the business community's social conscience, and the generous fund-raising (both corporate and personal) for cultural activities and social concerns. When the Dayton family elected to keep their huge department store downtown rather than moving it to the suburbs, it stimulated more than $200 million in new construction, reversing the familiar urban pattern of decay and turning the area into a bright and active commercial district. This is cited as an example of the public-spiritedness that gives the Twin Cities a sense of community, making it a welcoming and attractive place to live.

Minnesota's progressive political culture and its commitment to public education also helped create an open and optimistic environment that drew diverse groups of people to our state as a land of opportunity. Arthur Naftalin, a brilliant mayor of Minneapolis during the 1960s, points out that no single group— ethnic, religious, or business—has ever been able to take control of the state: "With our great variety, we have always had to form coalitions."

During the 1970 gubernatorial campaign, Democrat Wendell Anderson took a big political gamble and endorsed a tax-reform program. The plan called for the state to take over a large share of the school-financing burden from local districts, thus mandating a huge increase in the state budget. "The Republicans thought that Anderson had blundered fatally. That they were wrong is an excellent example of the sophistication of the Minnesota voters. They were willing to elect a man who promised to raise some of their taxes in return for larger overall gains." This major piece of social legislation, often referred to as the "Minnesota Miracle," significantly increased state aid for education and went a long way toward equalizing education in the cities, suburbs, and rural areas. It survived relatively unchanged for more than thirty years, until 2002, when the property tax structure was again revised by legislative action.

The article ends by acknowledging that other states have more dramatic attractions, of course. But there is something in the verdict of advertising executive Chuck Ruhr, who observes, "California is the flashy blonde you like to take out once or twice. Minnesota is the girl you want to marry."

This synopsis of the good life confirms what both native Minnesotans and those of us who have adopted the Twin Cities as our home already know: Minnesota is a great place to live. But our quality of life isn't static, and change is constant. There are always new problems to be addressed and solved. One of the reasons the Twin Cities continues to thrive is because its citizens don't leave things to other people. They roll up their sleeves, stand up for their ideals, and do what needs to be done.

For Seitz that meant reaching out to the business community and the public to explain good design and its potential to enrich our lives. Advocacy and education were his life's work.

Midwestern Modernism

For Seitz the language of good design was rooted in modernism, the once-revolutionary visual language that set the style for twentieth-century graphic design. Modernism has now become such an integral part of our everyday lives it is hard to imagine a time when it wasn't part of our environment. Thanks to the work and teaching of the many talented European cultural leaders who immigrated to the United States before, during, and after World War II, the ideas of modernism spread and influenced a generation of American designers.

According to design historian Lorraine Wild in her essay "Europeans in America," "During the 1930s the United States became the adopted home for many of Europe's most innovative designers, as an abbreviated list indicates: Alexey Brodovitch from Russia (1930); Joseph Binder from Austria (1930); Herbert Matter from Switzerland (1936); Gyorgy Kepes and Laszlo Moholy-Nagy from Hungary (1937); Will Burtin and Herbert Bayer from Germany (1938); Leo Lionni from Italy (1939). World War II brought over other designers as temporary visitors, such as A.M. Cassandre and Jean Carlu, both from France... . The vitality of the work created by the European designers and by the best of their American counterparts during the 1930s and 1940s is still admired and often referred to as 'timeless.' But in fact it is precisely because these designers responded to the ideas of their own time that their work looks so free and genuine."[6] The transfer of these visual characteristics (asymmetric layouts organized on an underlying grid system, the use of photography rather than illustration, and the exclusive use of sans serif typefaces) and ideas of European modernism became the intellectual foundation for a remarkable body of work by American designers and resulted in the emergence of the United States as an international leader in artistic innovation in the mid-twentieth century.

In the Midwest, the ideas of modernism were beginning to germinate among Twin Cities educators and designers such as Rob Roy Kelly, Dale Johnston, and Phil Mousseau when Seitz came to Minneapolis in 1964.[7] With Seitz's arrival, these advanced ideas in visual communication, which had developed in Europe at the Bauhaus and later at the Hochschule für Gestaltung (HfG) Ulm, became a more prominent part of Minnesota's cultural landscape. As a European immigrant, he became a direct link to the original ideas of European modernism. He developed a sophisticated, systematic style of graphic design at the Walker Art Center, and went on to form InterDesign, one of the first interdisciplinary design firms in the United States. His work reflected his deeply felt belief that business and the arts could be combined in service of the common good.

6. Lorraine Wild, "Europeans in America," in *Graphic Design in America: A Visual Language History*, ed. Mildred Friedman (exhibition catalogue) (Minneapolis: Walker Art Center: Minneapolis; and New York: Harry N. Abrams, 1989), 152–169.   7. Rob Roy Kelly, who graduated from the Yale School of Art in 1955, also preceded Seitz at the Walker Art Center, where he held a part-time position as design director. When Seitz arrived in Minneapolis in 1964, Kelly was chair of the design department at the Minneapolis School of Art. Dale Johnston studied with Kelly at MCAD, receiving a degree in graphic design in 1962. Johnston cofounded Design Center, one of the first graphic design firms in the Twin Cities, with John Reger, in 1969. Phil Mousseau also studied with Kelly at MCAD and graduated with a degree in graphic design in 1963. He went on to start the graphic design program at Minnesota State University Moorhead, where he taught several local design luminaries including Kenton Hanson, Mike Haug, Richelle Huff, Haley Johnson, Jeff Johnson, Gayle Jorgens, Mark Kraemer, Tim Larsen, Bill Pflipsen, Mike Skjei, Stan Wei, and Sharon Werner.

He was always looking for opportunities to improve the visual environment in the Twin Cities through good design.

In a 1950 article looking at the history of design from 1750 to 1950 published in the Walker's *Everyday Art Quarterly* (the predecessor to *Design Quarterly*), "good design" is premised on the classic modernist maxims of "form follows function" and "truth in materials."[8] Both concepts sought to distance the idea of design as a matter of styling—applying historical motifs to new products or using ersatz materials or techniques. Design was defined instead as a matter of "problem-solving," examining a specific problem and locating within it an appropriate solution. Although the term "good design" has a more precise and legitimate connection with the design of objects, its central principles were adopted by graphic designers. The function of a piece of graphic design was therefore connected to the clarity and legibility of its message, while its visual form was an expression of current printing techniques and technologies.

In the 1960s, American design came of age with great exuberance and unabashed enthusiasm. Graphic design had grown out of its trade status as a "commercial art" into a profession that met a wide variety of needs for a wide variety of clients. The objective rationality of modernism was particularly well suited for the corporate and institutional need for organized and consistent design systems.

At the same time, Minnesota had many corporations and cultural institutions with the resources and foresight to fund large-scale, comprehensive, interdisciplinary design programs. As a result, Seitz was able to use the conceptual clarity of modernism to create memorable identities and signage systems for such clients as the Minnesota Zoo, the Minneapolis Parkway System, the Minneapolis Convention Center, the Minnesota State Capital, the St. Paul Skyways, the Mayo Clinic, and the City of Des Moines as well as corporate identity systems for several Fortune 500 companies.

Community Design Center

In the tumultuous 1960s, volatile issues such as the civil rights movement, the women's movement, and antiwar movement divided the younger and older generations. This troubled decade, filled with anxiety and sweeping social changes, transformed our country in part by fostering a grassroots movement of social activism that challenged the vested interests of political, cultural, and religious authority. There was a genuine sense of idealism, a hope that social problems could be solved and justice would prevail. Many people, including local designers like Seitz, were motivated to develop meaningful solutions to communication problems and improve the community through design.

In the field of graphic design, the ideals of modernism also led

8. Hilde Reiss, ed., "The Tradition in Good Design," *Everyday Art Quarterly* 15 (Summer 1950): 13.

THE NEED FOR A COMMUNITY DESIGN CENTER

Disadvantaged, low-income and minority neighborhoods of the community are in need of professional design services as they seek to improve their environment and their way of life. These services normally are out of their reach.

The concept of a Community Design Center is based on this need, and on the belief that concerned professionals from the fields of environmental design desire to come together to help meet the need on a voluntary, non-profit basis.

These professionals will act together because of their interest in the quality of community design and their concern for the upward striving of disadvantaged and minority groups.

Furthermore, from time to time there are vital community issues which require, yet do not receive, design services because of shortage of funds or personnel. At present, there is no central place where concerned design professionals may come together to express their concern and offer their voluntary assistances.

Community Design Centers are now in existence in most metro- politan areas. Their activities and their specific structures are as varied as the demands and needs of their respective communities, but most work in low income neighborhoods and are involved with community action programs. The Community Design Center of Minnesota hopes to provide this service in our community, and in addition, become a educational center and focal point for all of the design professions in the area.

I

Excerpt from original proposal for the
Community Design Center, 1970

to the enthusiastic embrace of its clean aesthetic as a viable alternative to the visual clutter that was prevalent at the time. Massimo Vignelli, founder of the Unimark design firm in Chicago, explains, "The ethics of modernism, or I should say the ideology of Modernism, was an ideology of the fight, the ongoing battle to combat all the wrongs developed by industrialization during the last century. Modernism was a commitment against greed, commercialization, exploitation, vulgarization, and cheapness. Modernism was and still is the search for the truth, the search for integrity, the search for cultural stimulation and enrichment of the mind. Modernism was never a style, but an attitude."[9]

When Seitz was a student at the HfG Ulm, he was taught that designers have a responsibility to take an active role in society. The school advocated an objective and socially aware approach to design. Having personally witnessed the devastation of Europe during World War II, he developed a firmly held belief that designers can solve social as well as aesthetic and utilitarian problems. In the words of his teacher and mentor Otl Aicher, "We were interested in shaping the gestaltung, of everyday life and the human environment: we were interested in the products of industry and the attitudes of society. We refused to accept any longer that creativity should be classified according to its object."[10]

After he left the Walker Art Center in 1968, Seitz helped organize a design cooperative called the Community Design Center (CDC). Other members of this innovative nonprofit organization's board of directors were local architecture notables Roger Clemence, Alfred French, Bob Hysell, Roger B. Martin, Milo Thompson, and Duane Thorbeck.[11] The CDC enabled local graphic designers, landscape designers, and architects to collaborate and provide pro bono services for social causes in the Twin Cities area. Clemence points out, "This idea of a community design center was born out of a concern for social equity. We wanted to work in struggling communities, helping those less fortunate find professional design services to help them get their neighborhoods in shape. Peter helped reshape a community's understanding of what could be done."[12]

One of their first projects was for The Way, an outreach center for the North Minneapolis community. Members of the Community Design Center helped transform a vandalized vacant storefront at 1913 Plymouth Avenue into an attractive, safe, and functional meeting place for local residents. The building included a drop-in teen center with gym equipment and a portable boxing ring, a library, meeting rooms, offices, and a kitchen.[13]

The Designer as Teacher

In 1971, while working full-time as a partner at InterDesign, Seitz was hired by the Minneapolis College of Art and Design (MCAD) to teach the third-year graphic design class. Although it was a logistical challenge, he strongly believed that it was important for practicing designers to teach students the concepts and

9. Massimo Vignelli, "Long Live Modernism," *AIGA Journal of Graphic Design* 9 (1991): 1.   10. See Herbert Lindinger, ed., *Ulm Design: The Morality of Objects*, trans. David Britt (Cambridge, Massachusetts: MIT Press, 1991), 124–129.   11. French, Martin, and Thorbeck also joined Seitz in founding InterDesign.   12. Interview with Roger Clemence, September 21, 2007   13. See Dick Cunningham, "Community Center Nears Completion," *Minneapolis Tribune*, June 12, 1967.

Peter Seitz directing a client meeting with Minnesota Mutual, 1983

skills necessary to excel in the graphic design profession. It was also a meaningful way for him to share his hard-earned experience and give something back to the community: "I teach to pay back many things I got from my teachers and also to take care of our profession."[14]

Following in the footsteps of those illustrious designers who taught at the HfG Ulm (Otl Aicher, Max Bill, and Tomás Maldonado) and the graduate graphic design program at the Yale University School of Art (Norman Ives, Herbert Matter, Paul Rand, and Bradbury Thompson), Seitz introduced his students to the rigorous discipline and formal harmony of modern design. He once told me, "I don't believe in style, I believe in problem solving." He never missed a chance to emphasize the value of good design and how it influences ways that average people are informed. With passionate conviction, he often told his students, "Graphic design truly affects the everyday lives of people. As graphic designers, you have a real responsibility for protecting and enhancing our visual environment!"

A sampling of Seitz's former students and colleagues at MCAD comment on their experiences in his classes and at the college.

Monica Little (Class of 1978), Little & Company
"Peter focused on a very disciplined approach to problem solving. He never spoke theoretically. I was very impressed with his professionalism in the classroom as well as his professional success.

"His class was a window into the real design world where professionalism trumped the 'hippie craft' approach to design that was prevalent at the time. He taught his students to think of themselves as professional designers. But his dispassionate approach to class critiques was emotionally difficult for many students. His teaching method was painful but effective. I'm not sure that I would be a designer today if it wasn't for him.

"When Debra Cohen and I asked him for advice when we were thinking of starting our own business right out of art school, he didn't laugh at us! He counseled us in a 'big picture' sort of way. He emphasized that we would be communicating with business leaders and that our job was to help them understand how to do business with designers. We were bridging the gap between the business and design worlds."

Todd Nesser (Class of 1979), Larsen Design
"Peter brought a lot of energy to his classes. I remember that he focused on practical design problems with lots of critique time. He was tough but fair."

The following excerpt is from a letter by Nesser to Seitz congratulating him on his AIGA Fellow Award: "When I was a student in your third-year class, I was working a full-time snow plowing job at night. One day I arrived at your class exhausted

14. Seitz, in an interview by Karin Winegar, "Signer of Our Times," *Star Tribune*, August 27, 1997.

Peter Seitz with graphic design students at the Minneapolis College of
Art and Design, 1986

left to right: Hazel Gamec, Peter Seitz, and Patrick Whitney (MCAD Design
Department Chairman) in the faculty offices of the Minneapolis College of
Art and Design, 1980

and unprepared. Your response to my incomplete assignment was quick and to the point. 'Complete your assignment or don't come back.' I was embarrassed and angry, but I knew you were right.

"I quit my job, begged my parents for money, applied for student loans, and moved near campus to seriously study design. Although I am not the most successful of your many students, I am successful. In hindsight, I realize what a gift it was for you to push me to focus on my design studies. I could still be driving that snowplow. For that I am deeply grateful."

Charles Spencer Anderson (Class of 1981), CSA Design
"Peter's reputation definitely preceded him. He was larger than life, a demanding perfectionist with the knowledge, skill, background, and credentials to back it up. His authoritative approach, reinforced with a German accent and official mannerisms, was certainly intimidating at first. Later, when we saw him crack a smile or two and show genuine caring for his students' progress, we realized he had our best interests at heart.

"He emphasized that design was not merely a job, but a calling, a way of life, and a way to look at and engage the world. A famous Peter Seitz quote was, 'You must do these things in order to do them!' It was twenty years later, while watching a Nike commercial, that it suddenly occurred to me what Peter had actually meant. You have to make it happen! You have to be bold. You have to believe in your design and in yourself. Nike neatly summed up Peter's quote in three words: 'Just do it.'"

Jerry Stenback (Class of 1982), freelance designer
"Peter was on sabbatical during my third year at MCAD, but I did a work-study program with him and was an intern at Seitz Yamamoto Moss. As an employer and mentor, he was very supportive of my career in graphic design. He always insisted that I have a five-year plan.

"He had an air about him that commanded respect and loyalty. He offered excellent advice and showed me how to be a professional. He also taught me to respect my clients and to command their respect in return."

Jo Davison (Class of 1982), Larsen Design
"He challenged me to deal with the obstacles I faced with long-term rather than short-term goals, which is very hard to do. He made me cry. But I knew that he had my best interests in mind. His approach to problem solving had a profound effect on my life."

"He was an excellent role model, a true professional. Through his example, I learned about modernist values. He taught me that I always should be learning."

**Peter Chan (Class of 1986), Assistant Professor
at The Ohio State University**
"Peter's classes always focused on design problem solving.
He taught me to think broadly about the client's problem and
the user's perception. He emphasized that students should
never fall in love with their first design solution. We should
always try to do better."

Pam Arnold, MCAD DesignWorks Director
"I came to MCAD as an already degreed student. So, for me,
Peter's classes offered a welcome contrast to the theory
and methods driven curriculum of the 1980s. Peter brought
experience from his professional design practice to each
assignment. He walked his talk, showed us the way, and
encouraged us to design our lives. Peter essentially brought
the hopeful vision of the Bauhaus and Ulm to MCAD.

"I was completely enamored with Peter's interdisciplinary
design studio, InterDesign, which seemed to be a modern design
utopia. It inspired me to apply for the position of coordinator
at MCAD's own interdisciplinary in-house studio program,
DesignWorks (where I continue to work). It was a thrill for me
to develop a studio program where MCAD students could
practice design (work on real design projects), while pursuing
their design education. I felt like I was implementing the design
ideas and ideals Peter taught. To me, DesignWorks is the full
flowering of Peter's visionary approach to design education. I am
honored and proud to be a part of such a worthy effort to make
our little corner of the world better through design."

Kristen McDougall, former MCAD Design Department Chair
"Peter was my first exposure to a real design master. I was in awe
of him, and was motivated and inspired by his consummate
professionalism. His teaching was such a gift to MCAD and the
entire design community. For a design professional of his stature
to carve out the time to teach design students year in and year out
was amazing. He was always prepared, organized, and punctual.

"He challenged me, encouraged me, and advised me. I
particularly felt his impact as I passed through so many
institutions where Peter had left his mark (Yale, the Walker
Art Center, and MCAD). He was always available to share his
experience. When I was design department chair, Peter was a
valuable confidant. I always appreciated his forthrightness.
You always knew where you stood with Peter."

Russ Mroczek, MCAD Design Professor
"I first met Peter almost forty years ago while I was working in
Boston. He was design curator at the Walker Art Center at that
time, and I remember that he was one of the first to be aware
of the potential role of the computer in design and design
education. During his tenure at MCAD, Peter was a pivotal
faculty member in design, both in the professional world and
in education. He stood for professionalism in education."

Peter Seitz, 1984

Kevin Byrne, MCAD Design Professor

"Though Peter is recognized far and wide as a preeminent master teacher, I always felt he regarded his former students as peers. Often this was the process of evolution: many went from being Peter's students, to his protégés, to his peers. Most of his students eventually started their own businesses and studios. As a teacher and mentor, he has never turned down a request to meet an alum for coffee. I encourage you to do this. Bring your questions. You will discover that there is no question he will not at least try to answer, or as often, help you contextualize so you can answer it yourself!"

Hazel Gamec, MCAD Design Professor Emeritus

"I have so many memories about Peter in the twenty plus years we taught together at MCAD. I will always be grateful to him for the letters he sent to the MCAD faculty committee recommending my appointment as a professor in the design department. Thanks to Peter's advocacy on my behalf, I became the first woman professor in MCAD's history. This was an incredibly important milestone in my life. Many years later, thanks again to Peter's steadfast support, I became MCAD's first woman professor emeritus."

Seitz, who retired from teaching at MCAD in 2002, reflects on his thirty-year teaching career: "I'm sorry to say that I used to be a terrifying teacher. Too often I was unnecessarily harsh. However, my intensity was based on my belief that design was a serious business and my students must be serious about their studies if they were to succeed. I am still a modernist at heart, but I now know that there is more than one way to create good design. You might say that I'm a recovering perfectionist."[15]

As an educator, he was a taskmaster committed to quality design education and a compassionate mentor who took pride in the success of his students. During his years of teaching, including two terms as chair of the MCAD design department, Seitz influenced scores of gifted designers who went on to adapt the visual language of modernism into innovative new approaches for solving design problems.[16] His passion for precision and simplicity continues to inspire his students—now accomplished, well-respected designers with savvy business acumen—to strive for the highest standards of excellence in design.

The Computer Graphics Community

The close relationship between design, science, and technology was emphasized repeatedly during Seitz's studies at HfG Ulm. He brought this concept with him to the Walker Art Center, where he became one of the first design professionals to make the connection between emerging computer technology and its application to graphic design. In 1967, he designed and edited a landmark double-issue of *Design Quarterly 66/67* that featured the topic "Design and the Computer" [pages 104 and 105]. It was the first time the idea of using the computer as a design tool was discussed in a national design journal (in language

15. Interview with Peter Seitz, December 6, 2002.   16. In addition to those quoted here, Seitz also taught other respected and successful designers, including Nancy and Scott Baker (Baker & Associates), Debra Cohen (Debra Cohen Design), Cindy Fern Lamb (Lamb Art Direction), Minda Gralnek (Target Corporation), Dan Jurgens (StoryWorks Inc.), Ann Merrill (Larsen Design), Dan Olson (Duffy & Partners), David Peterson (Peterson Milla Hooks), Barbara Schubring (YWCA of Minneapolis), and Wayne Talley (formerly of FAME), to name a few.

Computer lab and typesetting equipment at the
Minneapolis College of Art and Design, 1984

that people other than computer scientists and engineers could understand).

Beginning in 1981, he spent three years setting up a state-of-the-art computer laboratory at MCAD. Thanks to his business contacts, he was able to secure donations of expensive systems that would have otherwise been unaffordable. In the early years, there were two labs. One contained a few Apple computers, a brand new Macintosh, and other small machines that were used to introduce students to basic computer capabilities. The other room was for advanced students and had the heavy duty, professional equipment, including three dedicated computer-graphics systems: a Dicomed D38, a Florida Computer Graphics system, and a 3M BFA Paint system.

The early 1980s were the dawn of what we now call "the personal computer revolution." Technology was constantly changing at an unprecedented, mind-boggling pace. Carol (Stenborg) Zen, who was hired by Seitz to teach computer graphics classes at MCAD, says of those early days, "Most of us who rode the beginning of that digital wave remember the constant 'hold on to your hat' sensation. But in the midst of this technological frenzy, Peter had the microcosm-macrocosm vision to anticipate future computer applications and skillfully integrate the teaching of graphic design and computer graphics in such a way that students never confused the tool with the design process."[17]

"Apple Computer's 1984 introduction of the Macintosh was a watershed event for the graphic design community," recalls Zen. "This little white machine with a smile was more than a personal computer, and much more affordable than the dedicated workstations." (The first Macintosh, introduced in January 1984, sold for about $2,495—more than $4,000 in today's dollars.) For the first time, a digital tool was made available to more designers and artists than ever before. Many of today's graphic design professionals recall that their first computer was a Macintosh. But the implications of this tool were much more profound, as Zen relates, "It is not just the Macintosh but many factors revolutionized the method, craft, and structure of design and illustration practices. These amazing technological advances changed design more than anything since the invention of the printing press. These are the tools that took design from the industrial age to the digital age. Today over 90 percent of design production and printing involves the Macintosh platform, along with software such as Adobe Photoshop, Illustrator, and InDesign."

Seitz saw the implications of the coming digital age and was responsible for not only bringing the first digital tools to MCAD, but also for shaping design curriculum that incorporated computers. He hired the most technologically skilled technicians to configure the innovative new lab and teach MCAD students the programs necessary to use the computer as an effective graphic design tool.[18]

17. Quotes in this and the following paragraphs are from an interview with Carol (Stenborg) Zen, August 17, 2007. 18. Miriam Edwards, Nancy Rowe, Pat Runyon, and Zen were among the first computer graphics teachers and lab technicians at MCAD.

When the Twin Cities hosted the SIGGRAPH (Special Interest Group for Computer Graphics) Conference in 1984, it attracted computer wizards from around the world. Even George Lucas (and his then-girlfriend Linda Ronstadt) showed up. More than twenty thousand attendees attended twenty-eight different classes as well as nearly forty different technical presentations. It made history as the largest conference ever held in Minneapolis up to that time. Co-chairs Dick Mueller and Dick Weinberg hired Seitz Yamamoto Moss to design the logo (page 159), promotional materials, and signage for the conference.

Mueller recalls, "I asked Peter to design a logo that had a sense of the future. It would be used in print and on screen, in two and three dimensions, in various sizes, and various media. It was one complicated design problem! He solved it by creating a simply elegant logo design with a perfect color scheme. It worked beautifully in all its different applications." Zen, who was Mueller's administrative assistant for the conference, adds, "For me, that logo design, like Peter's impeccably tailored suits, epitomized the understated elegance that is Peter."

Seitz also brought MCAD into the international SIGGRAPH limelight by organizing a juried show of computer graphics in its gallery. This was significant because it was the first time computer graphics were viewed not strictly from a business perspective, but held to artistic standards. It was wildly popular with conference attendees as well as the general public. This was the first time many Minnesotans had an opportunity to see computer-generated imagery firsthand and imagine the possibilities for this new medium of visual expression. The art show at the MCAD gallery, and the IMAX movie that premiered during SIGGRAPH, were accessible to the general public, whereas the majority of the conference presentations were highly technical, theoretical, and daunting to a general audience.

Professional Design Advocacy

Seitz's dedication to graphic design excellence is also reflected in his long-standing involvement with the graphic design profession. When Tim Larsen started making phone calls to create a list of graphic designers to influence the creation of a new graphic license plate by the State of Minnesota in 1976, Seitz agreed to lend his name to the list, *if* Larsen agreed to start a professional graphic design organization. He was instrumental in the founding of the Minnesota Graphic Designers Association (MGDA),[19] the predecessor of AIGA Minnesota, the local chapter of the professional association for design. He helped draft the MGDA Charter,[20] and served as the association's president from 1978 to 1979. He was a national board member of AIGA from 1983 to 1986, and has represented the Midwest for the Society of Environmental Graphic Designers (SEGD).

Seitz was the first Minnesotan to receive the AIGA Fellow Award in 2000. This prestigious award recognizes mature

[19.] Other designers who attended the first organizational meetings to form MGDA were: Bob De Bray, Bob Fleming, Jim Johnson, Sandy Johnson, Dale Johnston, Kevin Kuester, Tim Larsen, Eric Madsen, Phil Mosseau, Patrick Redmond, John Reger, and Bruce Willits. [20.] Excerpt from a news release dated March 1, 1977, announcing the formation of the Minnesota Graphic Designers Association: "MGDA will provide a forum for Minnesota graphic designers to speak out on public design issues, share professional information, develop high standards for the profession, and create public design awareness and understanding."

designers who have made a significant contribution to raising the standards of excellence in practice and conduct within the design community. Candidates are evaluated in the areas of education, writing, leadership, and reputation as well as the practice of design. At a gala dinner held in conjunction with the award on February 26, 2001, family, friends, and colleagues from around the world gathered to honor the patriarch of Minnesota graphic design.

The following comments from some of his many admirers offer further insights into the far-reaching influence Seitz has had on the Minnesota design community.

Tim Larsen, former MGDA President, Larsen Design
"When I think of Peter, the first word that comes to mind is 'generous.' Peter was generous with his knowledge and generous with his reputation. He was willing to risk both to help others."

Dale Johnston, former MGDA President, Design Center
"Graphic design was not a common term in the early 1960s. Yale graduates like Rob Roy Kelly and Peter Seitz were instrumental in increasing the visibility of the graphic design profession (as opposed to advertising) in the Twin Cities during that time.

"Peter's impeccable academic credentials were highly respected. He took his responsibility for promoting the value of good design very seriously."

Jim Johnson, former MGDA President
"I first met Peter at InterDesign just after I graduated from the Minneapolis School of Art. It was like meeting the Dalai Lama of graphic design. Peter was and still is the most disciplined man of integrity I know. I am proud to call him my friend."

Eric Madsen, The Office of Eric Madsen
"The one word I associate with Peter is 'professionalism.' I particularly respect and appreciate his pivotal role in raising the standards of design in our community on two levels. First, he educated our local corporate client base about the vital role professional design could play as a strategic business tool; and second, within our own profession, he raised the standards in design education.

"And then there is the accent. I could never quite compete with that, even though I laid on the Texas drawl as thickly as I could. He just sounded like a designer."

Heather Olson, former MGDA President,
AIGA Director of Education, Larsen Design
"Peter is a pillar of strength in education, a technology visionary, a designer totally dedicated to his field, a leader to be admired and respected. You can always count on Peter to listen intently and to respectfully offer his words of wisdom."

Any worthwhile story is larger than one person. Peter Seitz's story is about how one individual profoundly affected the lives of so many, while improving the visual environment of the Twin Cities. By tapping into his memories as well as those of his students and colleagues who were there with him, we can see a clearer picture of Minnesota's design history and get a better sense of our zeitgeist.

In the end, the vibrant, creative culture we continue to enjoy in the Twin Cities today is a result of community building—the kind Peter Seitz did so well by connecting people, resources, and good design to make the everyday lives of ordinary people better. The ideas and ideals of modernism that he planted in the rich cultural soil of Minnesota have flourished, setting the standard for quality design in the Twin Cities—something that we have come to expect and, often, now take for granted. Thanks to Seitz's advocacy that "good design is good business," many more people now know that good design *creates* social and economic value in local, national, and global communities. That is something we can build on. And, that is his legacy.

Peter Seitz in the design studio at the Walker Art Center, circa 1965

1954–1961

Augsburg Academy of Arts
Hochschule für Gestaltung Ulm
Yale University

—

EBON
GSKR

CONSTRUCTA
BREIT-MAGER

ACDFHIJIL
MPTUVW
XYZ

BLATT ⑤ PFEITZ   1. SEMESTER

Typography exercise | 1954
Augsburg Academy of Arts

1 Color chart and grid | 1955
  Hochschule für Gestaltung Ulm

2 Color and tone exercise | 1956
  Hochschule für Gestaltung Ulm

kurs t. maldonado
peano-fläche
7   peter seitz

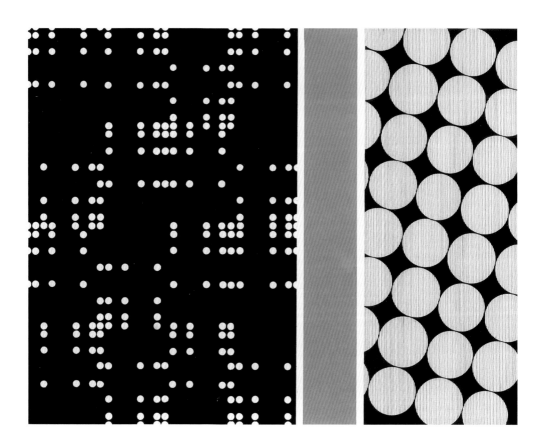

Tonal balance exercise | 1956
Hochschule für Gestaltung Ulm

Black as a Color | 1956
Hochschule für Gestaltung Ulm

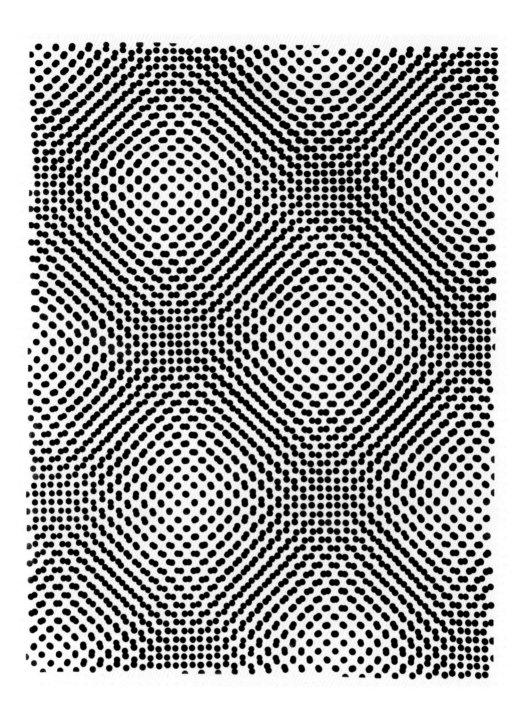

Exactness through Inexactness | 1956
Hochschule für Gestaltung Ulm

1 Kubus (children's block set) | 1956
Hochschule für Gestaltung Ulm

2 Rendering of Kubus packaging | 1956/2007
Hochschule für Gestaltung Ulm

Zur symptomatischen Grippebehandlung   # Fiobrol

Fiobrol dient zur Vorbeugung wie zur Behandlung
grippaler Infekte

J. R. Geigy AG   Basel

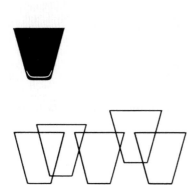

Gläser, Vasen

Um einen Raum wohnlich zu machen, ist es vorteilhaft,
wenn auch kleinere Gegenstände wie Blumenvasen, Gläser
und ähnliches vorhanden sind. Formschöne Gegenstände,
zum Beispiel auch Geschirr, Bestecke und Schalen, bringen
Abwechslung und Farbe in den Raum.

Behr Möbel GmbH Ulm-Donau
Glöcklerstraße 1 – 3   Ruf 3407

Behr Möbel

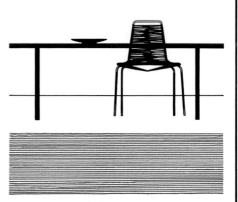

Dänische Möbel

Die skandinavischen Länder Dänemark, Schweden, Norwegen haben einen sehr starken Einfluß auf unsere Wohnkultur. Besonders Dänemark bringt uns sehr schöne Modelle. Die Vorliebe dieses Landes für edle Hölzer, insbesondere Teakholz, ist bekannt. Wir halten für Sie eine große Auswahl dänischer Möbel bereit.

Behr Möbel GmbH Ulm Glöcklerstraße 1-3

Behr Möbel

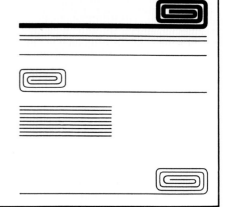

Teppiche und Dekorationsstoffe

bestimmen mit Material und Farbe den Charakter eines Raumes. Ausgesuchte Stoffdessins aus vielen Ländern, preiswerte Sisal- und Haargarnteppiche, Wollveloure und beste Handknüpfmuster zeigen wir in unserem vergrößerten Stoff- und Teppichraum.

 Behr Möbel GmbH Ulm-Donau
Glöcklerstraße 1-3   Ruf 3407

1 Advertisement for Behr Möbel, "Dänische Möbel" | 1957
  Hochschule für Gestaltung Ulm

2 Advertisement for Behr Möbel, "Teppiche und
  Dekorationsstoffe" | 1957
  Hochschule für Gestaltung Ulm

Bei Nässe, Schnee und Kälte sind ganz mit Lammfell gefütterte Après-Skischuhe warm und angenehm zu tragen. Besonders vorteilhaft sind die leichtgerippten und dadurch rutschfesten Sohlen dieser Modelle, die Sie in den verschiedensten Farb- und Lederkombinationen erhalten. Für den Skiläufer führen wir die bekannten und bewährten *Rieker* Skistiefel.

Ulm-Donau, Hirschstraße 16

Geiwitz advertisement,
"Après-Skischuhe" | 1957
Hochschule für Gestaltung Ulm

Edle Materialien werden für unsere Modelle verwendet und bringen somit Schönheit und Eleganz für Sie. Durch die klassisch-strenge Form, einen grazilen Absatz und eine schlanke Spitze, werden diese Schuhe zu einer Kostbarkeit für jede Frau.

Geiwitz

Ulm-Donau Hirschstraße 16

Die äußere, große Form und die Spitze entscheidet über die Eleganz eines Schuhes. Bei den Herren ist es die Art des Leders, ob glatt, genarbt, matt oder hochglänzend, und die Form der Spitze, ob rund, abgestumpft oder die neue „Carré"-Form, welche die besondere Freude an einem guten Schuh ausmacht.

Ulm-Donau, Hirschstraße 16

Der Spieltrog

ein neuartiger Sand- und Wasserspielplatz

Postwurfsendung

An alle **Bauunternehmungen**

Carl Götz GmbH
Neu-Ulm (Donau)
Telefon 93 44
Sperrholz · Furniere
Faserplatten · Türen

Ernst F. Hubert   Hochseefischerei und Tranfabrik, Kraftfutterwerk   Hamburg-Altona, Drestedt Krs. Harburg
Gegründet 1903   Medizinaltran Veterinärtran Technischer Tran   Chem. Pharm. Erzeugnisse Emulsionen Kraftfuttermittel

Telefon; 041862 (Treide) 206/207
Telegramm: Rohtran Buchholz Krs. Harburg
Postscheckkonto: Hamburg 11 76 70
Banken: Deutsch-Asiatische Bank, Hamburg
Spar-u.Darlehenskasse Hollenstedt e.G.m.b.H.

Ernst F. Hubert, Drestedt Bhf. über Buchholz Krs. Harburg

Ihr Zeichen   Ihre Nachricht vom   Unser Zeichen   Datum

Betrifft:

Ernst F. Hubert

Hochseefischerei · Tranfabrik · Kraftfutterwerk
Hamburg - Altona, Drestedt Kreis Harburg

Telefon: 041862 (Trelde) 206/207
Fabrikanschrift: Drestedt Kreis Harburg

Auftrag

Ich bestelle hiermit unter Einschluß der angegebenen Lieferungs-
und Zahlungsbedingungen:

Kg	Artikel	DM
	DM	

Lieferungstermine _____

Herr/Frau/Firma _____

Wohnort _____

Straße _____

Ort/Datum _____

Unterschrift des Käufers _____

Unterschrift des Vertreters _____

Die Preise verstehen sich einschließlich Verpackung, „frei Haus"
bzw. „frei Bahn- oder Poststation" des Käufers.

Nur die Vertreter mit Inkasso-Ausweis sind berechtigt, Beträge für
uns in Empfang zu nehmen. **bitte wenden**

1

auswirkungen dieser änderungen sind einsparungen an material, be-
arbeitungszeit, aufwand und eine erhöhung der sicherheit der arbeitsabläufe, welche durch vergleich und zeitstudien festgestellt und
bewertet werden können. änderungen in grösseren umfange (z.b. voll-
ständig neue arbeitsabläufe, einführung neuartiger maschinen u.ä.)
übersteigen zeit und möglichkeit des gestalters und sind einen
organisationsfachmann zu überlassen.

arbeitsablauf der produktionsreihe a nach neuorganisation:
schaubildliche darstellung:

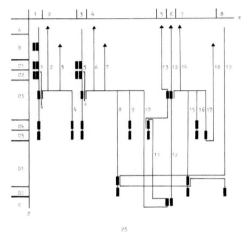

2

1 Forms design (order form) | 1958
  Hubert Fisheries

2 Systems-based graph for stationery components | 1958
  Hubert Fisheries

BRONISLAW MALINOWSKI

THE DYNAMICS OF CULTURE CHANGE

An Inquiry into Race Relations in Africa

A Yale Paperbound $1.45

The Dynamics of Culture Change (book cover) | 1960
Yale University Press

OPEN VISTAS

Philosophical Perspectives of Modern Science

HENRY MARGENAU

Open Vistas (book cover) | 1960
Yale University Press

MODERN FRENCH THEATRE

from Giraudoux to Beckett

JACQUES GUICHARNAUD
with June Beckelman

1964–1969

The Walker Art Center
The Guthrie Theater

1964 BIENNIAL
1964 BIENNIAL
OF
OF
PAINTING
PAINTING
AND
AND
SCULPTURE
SCULPTURE

WALKER ART CENTER

*1964 Biennial of Painting and
Sculpture* (exhibition catalogue) | 1964
Walker Art Center

98 **99**

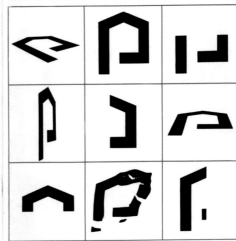

SIGNS AND SYMBOLS IN GRAPHIC COMMUNICATION

1) Athlete (woman)	
2) Cloak room	
3) Athlete (man)	
4) Press	
5) Shower	
6) Bath	
7) Sauna	
8) Press interview room	
9) Lunch room	
10) Dining room	
11) Lounge	
12) Bicycle depot	
13) Programs	
14) Telephone	
15) Shopping center	
16) Theater	
17) Ticket sale	
18) Dressing room	
19) Post office	
20) Camera	
21) Bus station	
22) Dispensary	
23) Band	
24) Guest room	

Sign languages for technical communication

As machines and equipment are exported from one language community into another, international sign systems for the operation of machines and equipment have become essential for the training and efficiency of operators. T. Maldonado and G. Bonsiepe have designed a "symbol system" for electronic data-processing machines and for displays and controls of electro-medical instruments. They first examined about 20 existing (technical) sign systems to find out if these systems offered any commonly accepted design constants. Then a sign "alphabet" containing the graphic equivalents of functional units of the equipment was made. These graphic signs corresponded to substantives of a language ("magnetic tape," "paper tape punch," etc.). Next a list of signs for the verbal equivalents of operations (verbs) and states (adjectives) was designed ("compare," "on-off," "ready," etc.). If necessary, these signs can be combined to indicate, for example, the state of a functional unit of equipment ("paper tape punch ready"). Because of their nonverbal character, such sign signs for technical communication transcend particular language communities and are easily learned. [19]

Top right:
Part of a new sign system for data-processing machines, designed for Olivetti by Tomas Maldonado and Gui Bonsiepe, Hochschule für Gestaltung, Ulm, Germany

Left:
Sign system for the Tokyo Olympics 1964: Pictographs identifying facilities, designed by K. Sugiura, I. Owatau, I. Tomaka, M. Katsumi and numerous Japanese graphic designers.

Below:
Sign system for data-processing machines by Tomas Maldonado and Gui Bonsiepe

a) functional unit	f) write	q) stop mistake due to jump
b) central unit	g) read	r) read magnetic tape
c) marginal unit	h) receive	s) accumulator at work
d) memory	i) trace	t) trace finished
e) magnetic tape	k) find	u) magnetic tape reading over
	l) mistake	
	m) on	
	n) off	
	o) over	
	p) blocked	

Left:
1) read
2) over
3) magnetic tape

Right:
magnetic tape reading over

25

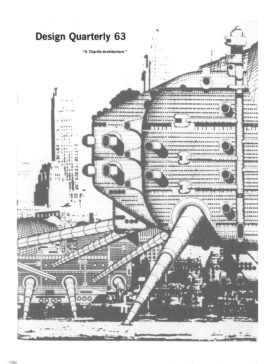

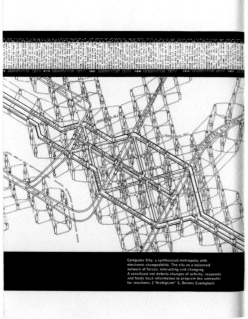

Computer City: a synthesized metropolis with electronic changeability. The city as a balanced network of forces, interacting and changing. A sensitized net detects changes of activity, responds and feeds back information to program the computer for reactions. ("Archigram" 5, Dennis Crompton)

The scarcity of examples of an "endless," or "indeterminate," architecture in the United States (almost none besides Eero Saarinen's Technical Center at General Motors exists) demonstrates that, at present, there is an unfortunate lack of interest here in architecture which is anonymous and not intended as monuments of individual self-expression.

In this issue of DESIGN QUARTERLY, Dr. Reyner Banham, critic, historian and longtime assistant editor of the renowned English magazine Architectural Review, presents an illustrated account of the development of "Clip-On Architecture" in England.　　　P.S.

A CLIP-ON ARCHITECTURE

Observers of the British design scene must have wondered what kind of architectural thinking may have emerged to parallel the rise of Pop and Op art in their London manifestations. The architects who are contemporary with pioneer Pop artists like Richard Hamilton are now well-known—James Stirling and James Gowan, for instance, are the 1965 winners of the Reynolds Aluminum prize and Alison and Peter Smithson will design the new British Embassy in Brasilia.

Those who fit into the mid-twenties to late-thirties age-bracket remained hidden from the public eye (because of the absence of finished buildings) until the Living City exhibition, sponsored by the Gulbenkian Foundation, at the London Institute of Contemporary Arts in 1963. This exhibition was organized and assembled by the team of architects and designers now known as the "Archigram Group," named after its irregular magazine Archigram. Like the exhibition, the recent issues of their magazine reveal an architectural vision—bright, mechanistic and big-city oriented—that is easily comparable with the visual language of painters like Peter Phillips, Derek Boshier and Joe Tilson. However, the quick comparison may too easily conceal the fact that this vision, which is shared in a different form by English architects like Cedric Price as well, stands upon a fairly deeply-rooted tradition of architectural speculation that goes back to 1950, or even further than that. Out of that tradition comes one cluster of speculative ideas that unites in the concept of an architecture of indeterminate form assembled from expendable components —the Clip-On or Plug-In concept.

3

The 13th Triennale

61

Design Quarterly

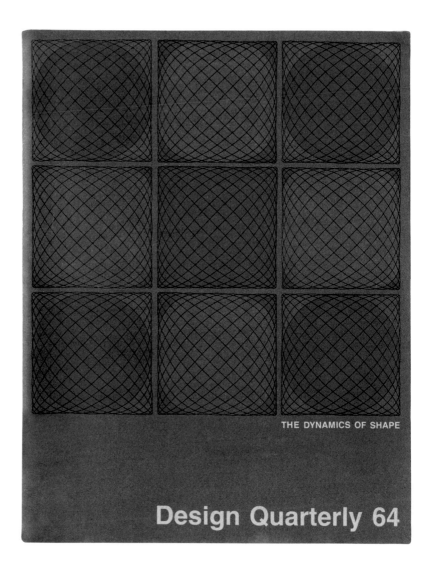

THE DYNAMICS OF SHAPE

Design Quarterly 64

DESIGN AND THE COMPUTER

Design Quarterly
66/67

Design Quarterly 66/67: Design and the Computer (cover and selected pages) | 1966
Walker Art Center

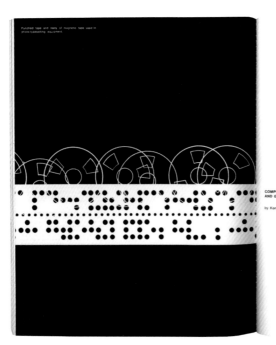

Punched tape and reels of magnetic tape used in photo-typesetting equipment.

Kenneth G. Scheid is president of K. G. Scheid and Associates, Pittsburgh, and formerly head of the Graphic Arts Department at the Carnegie Institute of Technology. He is interested in design education and the fundamental changes which are occurring in the design field today.

Scheid points out that publishers, editors, graphic designers, printers and typesetters are constantly being influenced by current developments in computer technology. It is now technically possible to establish systems in which the process of editing, setting type and printing is fully computerized. Newspapers and large publishing companies are most interested in these developments. Some papers in the United States already use systems where the reporter types out his story on an electric typewriter which simultaneously produces a tape for automatic typesetting. The editor's corrections are merged with the reporter's tape and fed to a computer which controls a phototypesetter or a linotype machine.

It is possible to produce systems where the editor sits in front of a television screen and calls up copy to appear on the screen, edits or deletes lines with an electronic stylus or light ray pen, then pushes a button causing the edited version of the copy to appear on the screen. He presses another button and the computer will have the type set and ready to print. Although this seems very futuristic, the elements for such systems are available, and as Mr. Scheid explains, work is being done which will change the functions and activities of the graphic designer, the typographer, the book designer and the layout artist.

In the very near future, graphic designers will have to concern themselves with these techniques, familiarize themselves with the technological possibilities and evaluate the aesthetic qualities involved.

COMPUTERS, PRINTING AND GRAPHIC DESIGN
by Kenneth G. Scheid

Printed communication can be achieved by means of an ever-widening variety of systems with modern technology. The most familiar one for capturing information in visual form is the typewriter, and the carbon copy process is very efficient in producing a limited number of useable duplicates. The camera is another common method especially useful for presenting nonverbal information, and photographic printing is a very efficient means of supplying a limited number of duplicates, provided that these copies are not needed instantaneously. A third familiar device is the printing press — ranging in scale from the office duplicator to massive newspaper and magazine units that permit virtually unlimited numbers of ink-on-paper copies to be produced rapidly and at low cost.

The selection of the most satisfactory system for a particular communications purpose and audience size, at any given stage of technological development, involves consideration of three major requirements:

1. Unit cost
2. Communications speed
3. Communications effectiveness

There is usually a trade-off among these factors. For example, a single letter will generally best be typed out on an office typewriter, at a unit cost of a dollar, in about fifteen minutes, with the design effectiveness that an individually-typed communication permits. However, when a letter should be copied a number of times, it will probably not be typed but run through a copying machine at an approximate cost of ten cents in less than a minute, because the communications effectiveness is entirely adequate compared to the cost of copy typing. Because of the fact that one might be willing to pay a slightly higher price for a graphically more effective result, a wide market has developed for the executive typewriter, which gives deep black, sharp and proportionally-spaced letter images. But no one is very likely to have the type for a single letter set and then printed, regardless of the quality of the result thus achieved.

To write the same letter to many persons, one would have to choose between typing each letter individually, duplicating an original and inserting personalized information, or typing automatically except for the manual insertion of the personalized material. The choice of process would be governed by the number of copies needed, equipment available, labor and time required, and the graphic effectiveness of each result.

Suppose, instead of a letter, a lengthy document which includes photographs and drawings — some even in color — has to be communicated to a large audience. Efficient printing systems for making thousands of copies would be offset lithography, gravure or letterpress printing. Here the type probably would be set in metal or by a photo-setting machine on film. The costs would be low — first, because the process permits the recording of far more information in a given area and thus economizes on paper, press time, binding time and mailing costs; second, the level of graphic effectiveness is highest; and third, despite a higher initial cost, the unit cost, when spread over thousands of copies, is comparatively low.

This example can be matched by numerous others. Cost, speed and design effectiveness govern the selection of systems for printing newspapers, journals and magazines of various circulations, advertising material, schedules, books, packages and business forms.

Rapid developments in computer technology have made improvements possible in the cost, speed and graphic effectiveness of printed communications. Some of the more important developments include the tape-punching typewriter, the tape-driven typewriter and typesetter, the magnetic or optical scanner, the high-speed chain printer, computerized typesetting employing the high-speed phototypesetter, computer-generated typesetting, versatile graphic arts film, the long-run offset plate,

53

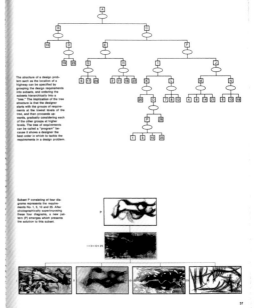

9 TRAVEL TIME

15 NOISE

21 CATCHMENT AREAS

10 PAVEMENT AND SUBGRADE COSTS

16 AIR POLLUTION

22 LOCAL ACCESSIBILITY AND INTEGRITY

11 DRAINAGE PATTERNS

17 WEATHER EFFECTS

23 FUTURE TRANSPORTATION SYSTEMS

12 BRIDGE COSTS

18 NON-RECOMPENSABLE PUBLIC AND PRIVATE LOSSES

24 EXISTING TRANSPORTATION SYSTEMS

13 LAND COSTS

19 PUBLIC FINANCIAL LOSSES

25 DUPLICATION OF FACILITIES

14 EYESORES

20 MAJOR CURRENT TRAFFIC DESIRES

26 SELF-INDUCED CONGESTION

26

The structure of a design problem such as the location of a highway can be specified by grouping the design requirements into subsets, and ordering the subsets hierarchically into a "tree." The implication of the tree structure is that the designer starts with the groups of requirements at the lowest levels of the tree, and then proceeds upwards, gradually considering each of the other groups at higher levels. The tree of requirements can be called a "program" because it shows a designer the best order in which to tackle the requirements in a design problem.

Subset P consisting of four diagrams represents the requirements No. 1, 3, 10 and 25. After photographically superimposing these four diagrams, a new pattern (P) emerges which presents the solution to this subset.

P

1 + 3 + 10 + 25

37

London: The New Scene

London: The New Scene

London: The New Scene

Peter Blake / Bernard Cohen / Harold Cohen / Robyn Denny / David Hockney / Howard Hodgkin
Allen Jones / Phillip King / Jeremy Moon / Bridget Riley / Richard Smith / Joe Tilson / William Tucker

London: The New Scene
(exhibition catalogue) | 1965
Walker Art Center

NICHOLAS KRUSHENICK

Nicholas Krushenick (exhibition catalogue) | 1968
Walker Art Center

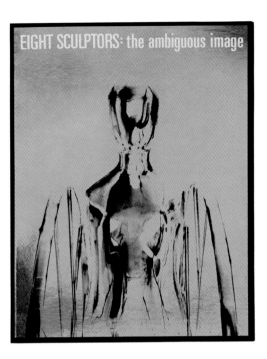

EIGHT SCULPTORS: the ambiguous image

CLAES OLDENBURG

Claes Oldenburg says, "I have a feeling that if I look at an object, I am doing something creative." The six works by Oldenburg in this exhibition are his creative-visions of everyday objects—an electric outlet, juicer, "Coke" ad, toilet, car engine and subway map. Oldenburg uses them as subjects representative of an environment he feels emphatic about and they are made into expressions of his ideas about these environments. The focus of attention in Oldenburg's work has progressively shifted from the street to the store to the home; to parts of the home—the bedroom, the kitchen and the bathroom; to the car and, most recently, back to the city. Such a sequential treatment continues to be an important aspect of Oldenburg's exploration of reality.

Oldenburg has the unique vision necessary to transform a banal subject into a meaningful image but the spectator sometimes needs preliminary knowledge, the clues, to "read" this imagery, to see the TOILET as a symbol of the mock sacredness of the bathroom, the SOFT ENGINE PARTS as an expression of nostalgia for the "air flow" Chrysler designs of the 1930s and the FALLING SHOESTRING POTATOES as an architectural landscape. Oldenburg concedes that the work of art must always remain something of a mystery. Although he brilliantly charges his forms with meaning, he explicitly states that the fantasy is in the eyes of the viewer. He does not want to "prejudice" the imagination any more than he wants to impose his fantasy too much on the object. He does not mind if interpretations differ about his work and allows that is meaning varies as it is seen in different environments. For all the specificity of subject matter, Oldenburg's works have a multiplicity of connotation.

Early in his career Oldenburg became dissatisfied with the spatial limitations of painting. His first three-dimensional objects of the late fifties had little depth and, in the spirit of assemblage, were made of scrap and found materials, all lacking in color. In 1961 an interest in new materials and full-color range developed when Oldenburg opened his "store"—a display in the artist's Lower East Side studio, of roughly modeled plaster images of food and clothing, painted in gaudy commercial hues. In 1962 he converted the same space into a performance area, the Ray Gun Theatre, and so set the stage for his first "Happenings." Oldenburg channeled much creative activity into the making of sets and properties for these events. The objects required had to be spatially impressive, yet resilient and light enough for the audience to be able to shove them around, bump into or to sit on them. These demands resulted in the production of his first "soft," oversized burlap and canvas objects stuffed with paper and rags.

In the current exhibition all works but the 1963

OUTLET WITH PLUG are "soft" objects. Whereas four pieces shown are made of raw or painted muslin, the 1965 SOFT JUICIT is executed in a brightly colored plastic-backed vinyl, which is the standard material for the final version of recent works. Claes Oldenburg is a prolific draughtsman, and each object in his sketchbooks passes through intricate metamorphoses which are triggered as much by the equivalence of forms in different objects as by the multiplicity of images contained within one form. A heavy paper mock-up, clipped and stapled together, is the first three-dimensional stage of a work. From this model, the artist's wife sews another version of canvas or muslin and this intermediate stage is dubbed the "ghost" to distinguish it from the final vinyl. Muslin versions not destined to be executed in vinyl may be dry-brushed in blacks, browns and grays. The result, as exemplified in SOFT ENGINE PARTS, can be a disarmingly "naïve" looking drawing, overlaying a "helpless" looking, semi-realistic form.

The affective power of Oldenburg's poetic transformations of the banal furnishings of the world we live in hinges on whatever aspect of reality he chooses to subvert. Things, like people, can become pathetic when taken out of familiar surroundings. Oldenburg realizes how much importance we attach to functionalism. Once he thwarts or removes it, its precise attributes turn into mockery. And if Oldenburg demonstrates how innocuous objects, when magnified, can become obstacles or menaces, he also shows how gigantic ones, reduced in proportion, can become precious or innocuous. Either way, the viewer is at a temporary loss to identify the subject. Because our sensory responses are conditioned by experience, a "soft" toilet or "hard" wedge of pie by Oldenburg shocks us out of routine acceptance of things at their face value. He affirms that "fooling" the viewer is part of his intention, and that a work can derive some of its power by frustrating our expectations.

Oldenburg believes that his objects belong to a realm halfway between the world of art and the world of real things. In his work, he stresses the ambiguity of the almost-but-not-quite that separates the reality of art from the reality of life. Oldenburg felt stimulated by the comments of visitors to the "store," some of whom said: "This is not art, it's a hamburger!" while others took the opposite position: "This is not a hamburger, it's art!" These reactions proved that he had been successful in raising questions in the viewer's mind. Oldenburg aspires to create another reality which shatters preconceptions and enables us to see with perspicacity the true complexity of reality.

The mode and degree of Oldenburg's intervention in the world of real objects are dependent on how these objects affect him. Oldenburg is highly

Eight Sculptors: The Ambiguous Image
(exhibition catalogue) | 1966
Walker Art Center

Pistoletto (exhibition catalogue) | 1967
Walker Art Center

1966 Biennial of Painting and Sculpture /
Sculpture / 1966 Biennial of Painting a
and Sculpture / 1966 Biennial o
Biennial of Painting and Sculpture
Sculpture / 1966 Biennial of Pa
of Painting and Sculpture / 1966
1966 Biennial of Painting and Scu
and Sculpture / 1966 Biennial of
Painting and Sculpture / 1966 Bienn
Biennial of Painting and Sculp
Sculpture // 1966 Biennial of Painti
of Painting and Sculpture / 1966
1966 Biennial of Painting an
and Sculpture / 1966 Biennial
Biennial of Painting and Sculpture /
1966 Biennial of Painting and S
and Sculpture / 1966 Biennial of
Biennial of Painting and Sculpture
1966 Biennial of Painting and Sc
Sculpture / 1966 Biennial of P
of Painting and Sculpture
Painting and Sculpture / 1966 Bien
of Painting and Sculpture / 196
1966 Biennial of Painting and Scu
and Sculpture / 1966 Biennial o
of Painting and Sculpture / 1966 Bie

1966 Biennial of Painting and Sculpture /
Walker Art Center / September 24 — October 30

*1966 Biennial of Painting and
Sculpture* (call for entries) | 1966
Walker Art Center

THE EXPRESSION OF GIO PONTI / AN EXHIBITION OF WORK BY THE MILANESE ARCHI-TECT-DESIGNER INCLUDING: BUSINESS, RESIDENTIAL, EDUCATIONAL, AND RELIGIOUS ARCHITECTURE; FURNITURE, GLASS, SILVERWARE, STAGE AND INDUSTRIAL DESIGN; CITY PLANNING, PAINTING AND DRAWING / JUNE 5 THROUGH JULY 9, 1967 / WALKER ART CENTER, 1710 LYNDALE AVENUE SOUTH, MINNEAPOLIS, MINNESOTA 55403.

The Expression of Gio Ponti
(exhibition invitation) | 1967
Walker Art Center

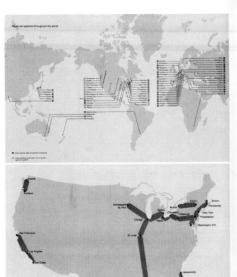

Exhibition design for *Mass Transit:*
Problem and Promise | 1968
Walker Art Center

1968 biennial of painting and sculpture /september 8 - october 13/ walker art center

1968 Biennial of Painting and Sculpture (poster) | 1968
Walker Art Center

walker art center
october 2 - november 10

hamilton/kitaj/paolozzi/tilson

prints
from
london
prints
from
london
prints
from
london
prints
from
london

Prints from London (poster) | 1968
Walker Art Center
Designed with Gay Beste Reineck

Design Quarterly 74/75: Process and Imagination
(cover and selected pages) | 1969
Walker Art Center
Designed with Gay Beste Reineck

DESIGN QUARTERLY 74/75
Editor: Christopher Finch
Art Direction: Interdesign Inc.
Editorial Assistant: Carol Collwell
Circulation: Gerrie Devine

Design Quarterly is indexed in Art Index.
Subscription rates are 4 issues $9.00, 8 issues $18.00, 12 issues $26.00.
Single issues $3.00. Double issues $5.00
Foreign postage $1.00 for 4 issues. Design Quarterly is published by
Walker Art Center, 201 Hennepin Avenue, Minneapolis, Minnesota 55403.

Change of address: To insure receiving all copies, give the old address as
well as the new one and attach the sticker for change to enclose effective.

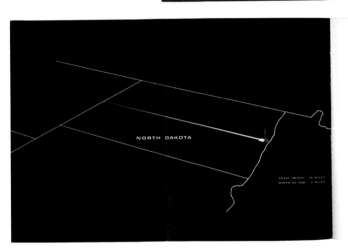

NORTH DAKOTA

TOTAL HEIGHT 18 MILES
WIDTH AT TOP 6 MILES

sia armajani

TOWER, NORTH DAKOTA

PROBLEM DEFINITION:
Specify a tower which will cast a shadow
across the entire state of North Dakota.

Good quality road maps show the average
width of North Dakota (East-West) to be about
360 miles. Thus, this is the maximum shadow
length required. If the earth were flat, a very
short tower would be sufficient.

However, curvature of the earth must be taken
into account. This requires that we compute
the angle subtended by North Dakota measured
from the center of the earth. This is a great
circle arc:

Average width of North Dakota = 360 miles
Approximate circumference of earth = 24,860
miles
Angle subtended by North Dakota = $2\pi \times \frac{360}{24,860}$
= .091 radians
= .091 × 57.3 degrees/radian
= 5.2°

Thus North Dakota subtends 5.2° on great circle.

Although North Dakota includes about seven
degrees of longitude (104 degrees to 97 degrees
West longitude), the great circle arc subtends
only 5.2 degrees. The closer we get to the
North Pole, the smaller great circle arc is
subtended by a seven degree difference in
longitude co-ordinates. With the assumption
of a smooth earth, i.e. no mountains, valleys,
etc., the trigonometry problem shown must
be solved.

OF MICE AND MEN
John Steinbeck

A MIDSUMMER NIGHT'S DREAM
William Shakespeare

THE RELAPSE
Sir John Vanbrugh

1972
GUTHRIE
THEATER
SEASON

AN ITALIAN STRAW HAT
Eugene Labiche and Marc-Michel

OEDIPUS THE KING
Sophocles/Anthony Burgess

THE GUTHRIE THEATER. Vineland Place. Minneapolis/Saint Paul, Minnesota. Michael Langham, Artistic Director

Guthrie Theater Season (poster) | 1972
Guthrie Theater
Illustration: Miranda Moss

Harpers Ferry (poster) | 1967
Guthrie Theater
Illustration: Miranda Moss

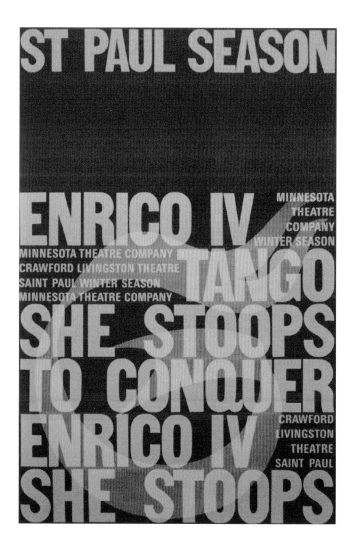

St. Paul Season (poster) | 1970
Minnesota Theatre Company
Designed with Gay Beste Reineck

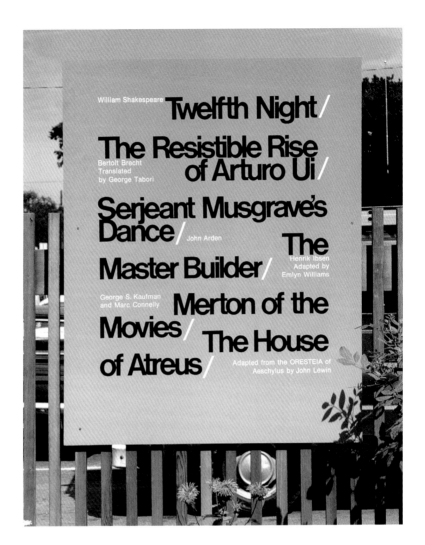

1969–1996

Visual Communications Inc.
InterDesign Inc.
Seitz Graphic Directions
Seitz Yamamoto Moss
Peter Seitz & Associates

InterDesign Inc.

InterDesign Inc. is a new firm organized to provide an interdisciplinary approach
to environmental design problems.
Through a team of professionals representing the areas of architecture,
urban design, planning, landscape architecture, engineering, visual communications,
industrial design and systems analysis, InterDesign Inc. is able to provide the
full range of professional services.

InterDesign Inc. / Minneapolis-Saint Paul / Minnesota

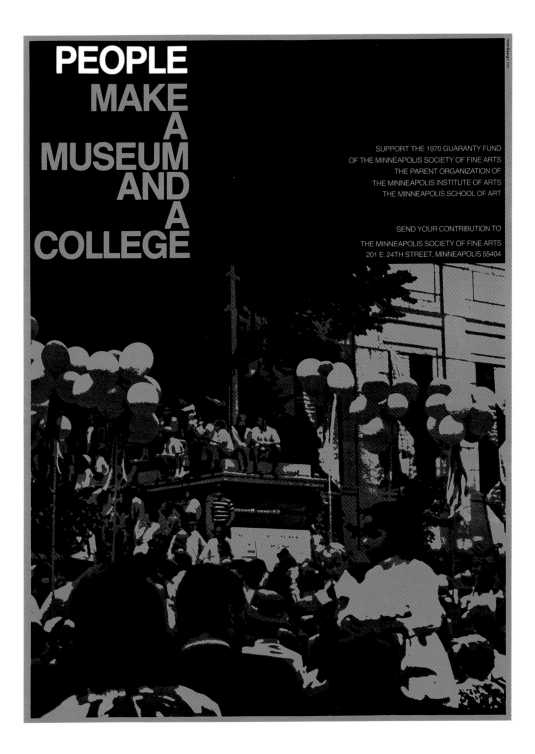

PEOPLE
MAKE
A
MUSEUM
AND
A
COLLEGE

SUPPORT THE 1970 GUARANTY FUND
OF THE MINNEAPOLIS SOCIETY OF FINE ARTS
THE PARENT ORGANIZATION OF
THE MINNEAPOLIS INSTITUTE OF ARTS
THE MINNEAPOLIS SCHOOL OF ART

SEND YOUR CONTRIBUTION TO
THE MINNEAPOLIS SOCIETY OF FINE ARTS
201 E. 24TH STREET, MINNEAPOLIS 55404

People Make a Museum
and a College (poster) | 1970
Minneapolis Society of Fine Arts
Designed with Gay Beste Reineck

First National Video Tape Festival
and Workshops (poster) | 1972
Minneapolis College of Art and Design

Saint John's University

Preparing
to meet the future...

Saint John's is a strong and viable private University with able, progressive leadership and a vibrant liberal studies program. With the help of many alumni and friends as well as corporations, government agencies and private foundations, the University has been able to maintain academic excellence and service to its communities. Equally important, however, has been Saint John's adherence to the principles of sound fiscal management. Year after year, despite continuing high inflation, the University has been able to achieve its goals of academic and professional education and community service within a balanced budget.

Saint John's is aware, however, that economic issues will be a major concern in the next decade. Spiraling costs, probable reduced state and federal funding, and the likelihood of competing with public colleges for fewer college-bound students are a few of the specific problems which will affect all of American higher education.

Efficient operation, accountability in all departments and careful planning have established a secure financial foundation for the University. The comprehensive, ongoing planning process has enabled Saint John's to remain academically and fiscally strong, and it has also permitted the University to focus on major spending priorities to assure future strength.

Saint John's future economic priorities have been carefully determined and reflect its commitment not merely to survive but to foster the distinguishing features of its educational program and the Benedictine heritage they represent.

The University's priority needs include:

1) Renovation of key campus buildings

2) Endowment for scholarships, faculty and visiting faculty chairs and for the Hill Monastic Manuscript Library

With confidence in its programs as well as its potential, Saint John's invites the partnership of others who share its commitment to the values of the 1,500-year-old Benedictine educational tradition.

Admissions catalogue | 1974
Saint John's University
Designed with Kevin Kuester

Northwest Architect

MAY/JUNE 1970

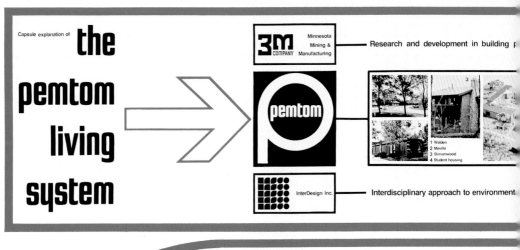

the pemtom living system

Capsule explanation of

3M COMPANY Minnesota Mining & Manufacturing — Research and development in building

pemtom

1 Walden
2 Movita
3 Birnamwood
4 Student housing

InterDesign Inc. — Interdisciplinary approach to environment

marketing

a variety of types of ownership through direct purchase, condominiums, cooperatives, rental and leasing will result in maximum buyer appeal

balanced communities

planned neighborhoods are feasible with the modular building concept which places emphasis on total environment rather than individual dwelling unit

management

site analysis, density requirements and individual project designs are coordinated with modern production control and marketing techniques to combine the benefits of mass production with desired qualities in the social and physical environment

superior quality

stressed skin construction with polymer bonding results in dwelling units of superior quality and easy maintenance

adaptability

system adapted for hot (120° F.) and cold (−40° F.) climates, wet and dry regions. Suitable for coastal areas

densities

compatible in rural, suburban and urban areas, design flexibility permits individual site design of varying densities

individuality

modular design and construction permits flexible planning, encourages individual decoration and "do it yourself" renovations

environmental adaptability

constraints/solutions

procedures to reduce the cost and increase the quality of housing

construction methods

the current archaic and fragmented methods of the construction industry must be replaced by a total building system, developed through the use of systems analysis and computer techniques

unions

new agreements to accept factory assembly of modular units through union supervision of fabrication process must be reached with the Building Trades

transportation

coordination on a National level to allow transportation of housing units up to 14' wide will increase the opportunity to achieve a desired environmental result

acceptance

public unfamiliarity and past rejection of prefabricated housing by municipal ordinances will require a promotional effort through prototype construction to demonstrate potential of total building systems

codes

national standards must be developed to allow innovative technology and

costs

through coordinated land development, financing, market-

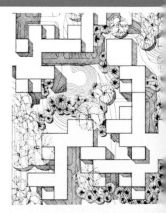

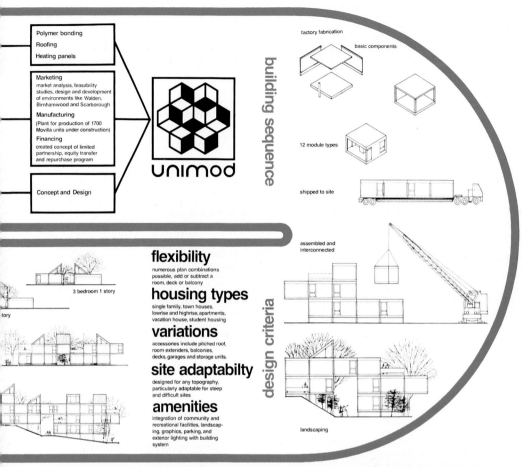

Polymer bonding
Roofing
Heating panels

Marketing
market analysis, feasability studies, design and development of environments like Walden, Birnhamwood and Scarborough

Manufacturing
(Plant for production of 1700 Movilla units under construction)

Financing
created concept of limited partnership, equity transfer and repurchase program

Concept and Design

unimod

factory fabrication

basic components

12 module types

shipped to site

assembled and interconnected

landscaping

3 bedroom 1 story

story

flexibility
numerous plan combinations possible, add or subtract a room, deck or balcony

housing types
single family, town houses, lowrise and highrise, apartments, vacation house, student housing

variations
accessories include pitched roof, room extenders, balconies, decks, garages and storage units.

site adaptabilty
designed for any topography, particularly adaptable for steep and difficult sites

amenities
integration of community and recreational facilities, landscaping, graphics, parking, and exterior lighting with building system

ing and mass produced factory fabricated housing units substantial improvements can be made to lower the cost and increase the availability of housing

time
the techniques of mass production substantially increase the rate as well as the volume of production, thus eliminating long lead times in planning and prolonged on-site construction. Computer control will minimize unnecessary delays due to material unavailability and delivery problems

financing
superior construction, lower costs and maintenance will reduce the mortgage costs and thus reduce the costs of home ownership

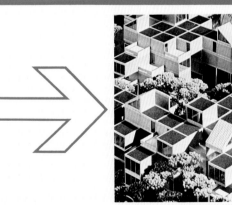

urban/regional studies institute

Urban and Regional Studies Institute
has been providing a dynamic interdisciplinary undergraduate and graduate program in the emerging areas of Urban and Regional Planning, Development, and Management since 1966.

Theme
The theme of the Institute is creative, applied problem solving, built upon individualized academic program design.

Program
The program is geared toward training the generalists rather than the specialist. These generalists will be the men and women who can direct and manage growth toward improving the quality, rather than the quantity, of life.

Involvement
The Institute emphasizes participatory community and regional involvement while providing innovative learning environments (such as computer simulation games and internship opportunities) as educational tools.

Employment
Almost unlimited employment opportunities exist for Institute graduates trained in a broad spectrum of planning and management skills.

Information
A brochure describing our program as well as a copy of this poster will be sent upon request to:

Director
Urban and Regional Studies Institute
Box 007, Mankato State College
Mankato, Minnesota 56001

Mankato State College
Mankato, Minnesota 56001

Winter Calendar (poster) | 1974
University of Minnesota

1970
summer
session
macalester
college

Two Four-week Terms
June 8 - July 3
July 6 - July 31

8 Semester Hours in 8 Weeks —
$30 Per Semester Hour

90 Courses in Art, Biology, Chemistry,
Classics, Economics, Education, English,
French, Geography, Geology, German,
History, Mathematics, Music, Philosophy,
Physical Education, Physics, Political
Science, Psychology, Religion, Russian,
Sociology, Spanish and Speech

Courses for Teacher Certification
or Refreshment

An Active Campus in an Enjoyable
Metropolitan Area

On the campus: Summer Theater
Concerts, Lectures . . . A Composer's and
Conductor's Workshop in 20th Century
Music . . . Institutes in General Science,
American Studies; Comparative Urban
Systems, Politics and Field Biology

Around the campus: A wide range of
opportunity for entertainment and recreation
. . . The Minnesota Symphony . . . Boating
and Fishing Lakes . . . Parks for Picnics . . .
The Guthrie Theater . . . The Minnesota
Twins . . . A Cosmopolitan Metropolitan Area

Send for a Catalog:
Director of Summer Programs
Macalester College
St. Paul, Minnesota 55101

Clip and mail to Director of Summer Programs
Macalester College, St. Paul, Minnesota 55101

Please send a summer school catalog to:

Name _____

Address _____

_____

Summer Session (poster) | 1970
Macalester College
Designed with Gay Beste Reineck

Designing a Life

celebrate trees

Minnesota Arbor Month: May '79

Minnesota Department of Agriculture, Room 600, Bremer Building, St. Paul, Minnesota 55101

Minnesota Arbor Month, "Celebrate Trees" (poster) | 1979
Minnesota Department of Agriculture
Designed with Hideki Yamamoto

THE
MINNEAPOLIS
SOCIETY
OF
FINE
ARTS
ANNUAL
REPORT
1969

Designing a Life

The Minneapolis Society of Fine
Arts Annual Report | 1969
Minneapolis Society of Fine Arts
Designed with Gay Beste Reineck

Financial Report 1972

UNIVERSITY OF MINNESOTA

Directional signage | 1971
Midwest Federal Savings and Loan

Modular exhibition system and exhibition design | 1973
Minnesota State Art Council

Pictographs for Minneapolis
Parkways System | 1976
Minneapolis Park Board
Designed with Hideki Yamamoto

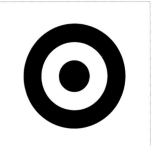

Northern Trek kiosk and signage | 1977
Minnesota Zoo

Tram graphics | 1976
Minnesota Zoo
Designed with Duane Thorbeck
and InterDesign Inc.

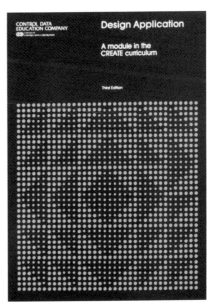

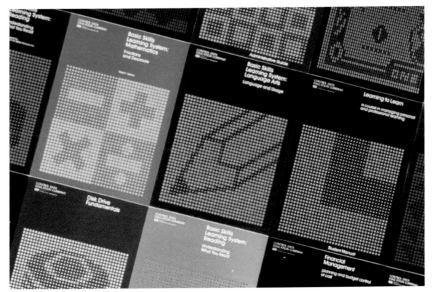

Design system and various cover designs
for CDC Learning System | 1978
Control Data Corporation

1 Stationery and identity materials | 1983
Minneapolis Children's Medical Center

2 Children's block set | 1983
Minneapolis Children's Medical Center
Designed with Miranda Moss

Minnesota Graphic Designers Association

The Minnesota
Graphic Designers
Association invites
design professionals
living and working
in the midwest area
to submit their work
for inclusion in the
MGDA Graphic
Design Show 1986

CALL
FOR
ENTRIES 1 9 8 6

1 Directional signage for Des Moines
  Skyway System | 1983
  City of Des Moines

2 Environmental graphics and
  signage design | 1988
  Pacifico Convention Center, Yokohama
  Designed with John Lees

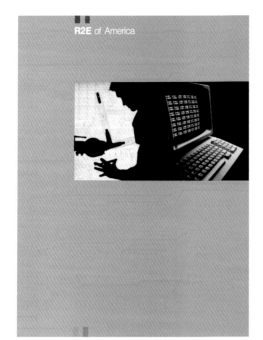

1 Brochure design | 1982
  R2E of America
  Designed with Miranda Moss

2 Brochure design | 1981
  Hammel, Green and Abrahamson,
  Architects and Engineers
  Designed with Hideki Yamamoto

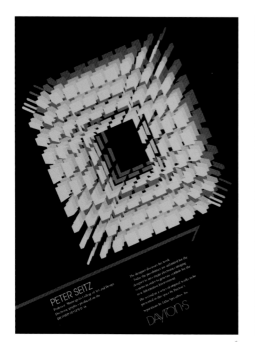

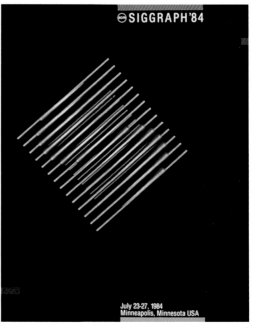

1

2

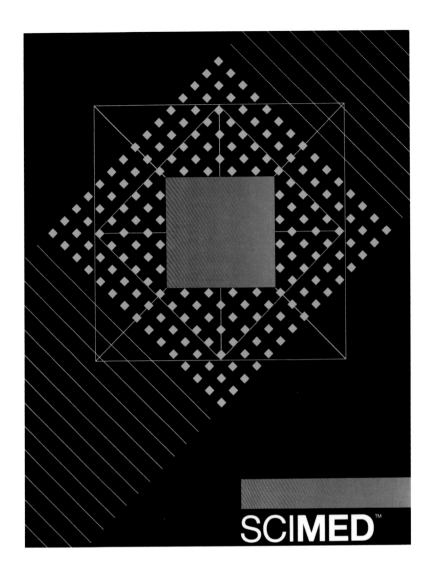

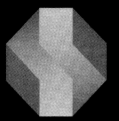

5

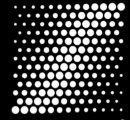

6

7

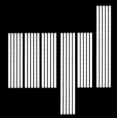

8

5 Integrity | 1990

6 Peter Seitz & Associates | 1988

7 State of Minnesota Agricultural Products | 1983

8 Minneapolis Public Library | 1970

9

10

11

12

9   Minnesota Mutual Life | 1977
    Designed with Hideki Yamamoto

10 St. Paul Skyways | 1970

11 Jefferson Buslines | 1973

12 Minnesota Zoo | 1976

13

14

15

16

13 Hazelden Treatment Center | 1989

14 Miracle Ear | 1981

15 Lutheran Brotherhood | 1977
   Designed with Hideki Yamamoto

16 Minneapolis Institute of Arts Centennial | 1980

17

18

19

20

21

22

23

24

21 SIGGRAPH | 1984

22 Dicomed | 1990

23 Gelco Corporation | 1979
   Designed with Hideki Yamamoto

24 Pinkard Realty | 1964

Peter Seitz in the InterDesign Inc. studio, 1972

Chronology

Compiled by Kolean Pitner

Origins and Influences

1931 Peter Seitz is born in Schwabmünchen, Germany (population 5,000), located fifteen miles south of Augsburg. He is the second of four sons of Olga (Kirschenhofer), a homemaker, and Georg, an employee for the local brewery Hasenbrau.

As a child, when he wasn't drawing, painting, or doing chores, Seitz read adventure stories, particularly the series of Wild West novels by German author Karl May. Each summer the Seitz boys (Wolfgang, Peter, Alois, and Georg) worked on their father's 65-acre family farm, which was

left: The Seitz family, 1948   right: Schwabmünchen, Germany, after Allied bombing, 1945

run by his aunts and uncles. The family hoped the farm would eventually be taken over by one of the boys; Georg remained there, but the other siblings pursued different interests.

1943 During World War II, Seitz's father is drafted into the German army and stationed at a nearby airstrip.

The city of Augsburg is firebombed.

1945 Bombs strike Schwabmünchen. Sixty people are killed and several hundred seriously injured. Though the Seitz home is spared when bad weather affected the targeting of the area, nearly 120 buildings are destroyed in the town. The war ends three months later.

1946 Since the two local schools were in ruins and his parents couldn't afford to send him to study elsewhere, Seitz is apprenticed to

local master painter Luipold Gogl from whom he learns sign painting and other techniques. He travels to Augsburg once a month for classroom instruction in his craft, where he excelled in hand lettering and painting decorative Germanic motifs such as the bands of floral designs popular for home interiors at that time.

1948 Seitz becomes a journeyman painter and continues to work for Gogl for five years.

1953 Seitz is introduced to a talented graphic designer and graduate of the Augsburg Academy or Arts who worked for the Augsburg opera house. Seitz considers seeing his work a definitive moment in his decision to become a graphic designer.

1954 Seitz begins his design studies at the Augsburg Academy or Arts. Author and

Cafeteria at the Hochschule für Gestaltung Ulm, Germany, circa 1956

calligrapher Eugene Nerdinger, director of the graphic arts department, is impressed with Seitz's work skills and recommends him for a position as a salesman and production artist at a local textile-engraving company. This job helped Seitz to expand his knowledge of the graphic arts, especially printing, and allowed him to learn more about possible career options while continuing his studies.

The Hochschule für Gestaltung Ulm (HfG Ulm) opens. Modeled after the Bauhaus, which was shut down by the Nazis in 1933, HfG Ulm is designed by Swiss architect Max Bill and dedicated to the daring and sacrifice of Hans and Sophie Scholl, two resistance fighters executed for printing anti-Nazi pamphlets and posters.

HfG Ulm was financed by the Scholl Foundation with gift funds from the United States and Norway, which guaranteed its academic independence. Its experimental approach to education was based on the optimistic belief that students would be involved in "the making of a new culture." An interdisciplinary approach to design was at the heart of the curriculum. The three main departments—architecture, visual communications, and product design—collaborated on a variety of projects.

The Ulm Years: A Modernist in the Making, 1955–1959
1955 On a Sunday morning in early summer, Seitz's mother shows him a newspaper article about a school of design with a beautiful new campus just outside Ulm. This glowing summary of HfG Ulm's successful first year inspires Seitz to ride his bicycle sixty miles to inquire about enrolling as a design student in the fall.

He is accepted as one of about thirty first-year students at HfG Ulm, where his studies begin with a yearlong foundation course of basic design studies and include classes in psychology, sociology, behavioral science, and marketing as it relates to design. Argentine designer Tomás Maldonado, one of Seitz's foundation teachers and mentors, was the first person to encourage him to consider a teaching career.

1956 Seitz befriends John Lottes, an American student from the Minneapolis School of Art studying at HfG Ulm on a Fulbright Scholarship, with whom he hones his English skills. For the first time, Seitz seriously considers working or studying in the United States.

HfG Ulm director Max Bill chooses Seitz to work with him on a poster and a new line of wallpaper designs for the Swiss company Sallubra. At the same time, a rift develops between Bill (a

Renaissance man who was considered part of "the old guard") and a group of students and faculty that wanted the school to take a more technological approach to design. Bill later resigns. Seitz had supported the director, and his scholarship is not renewed.

1957 Otl Aicher, another of Seitz's design teachers, hires him to work in his studio and becomes his most influential mentor. Aicher had recently been teaching and lecturing at Yale University, and he encourages Seitz to apply to Yale's graduate graphic design program.

1958 Seitz is accepted as a graduate student at Yale University's School of Art. Aicher's letter of recommendation for him results in a tuition scholarship from the university.

A runner-up for a Fulbright Scholarship to study at Yale, Seitz receives a $250 Fulbright Travel

Otl Aicher instructing a class at the Hochschule für Gestaltung Ulm, 1956

Grant from the American Women's Club at the Stuttgart Army Base.

1959 Seitz completes his senior thesis (a corporate identity for Hubert Fisheries in Hamburg, Germany) and graduates from HfG Ulm with a bachelor's degree in visual communication.

The Yale Years: American Finishing School, 1959–1961

Walter Zeischegg, a product design teacher at HfG Ulm, arranges for Seitz's free passage on a Danish freighter from Hamburg to Montreal. He arrives at Yale to begin his graduate studies several days after the fall semester begins.

At Yale, Seitz studies with such celebrated graphic designers as Paul Rand, Bradbury Thompson, and Norman Ives. He also studied photography with Swiss designer Herbert Matter.

1961 Seitz completes his thesis (a series of theater posters) and receives his MFA degree in graphic design and photography from Yale in the spring.

Martin Friedman, director of the Walker Art Center in Minneapolis, interviews Yale students for a designer and curator position. Seitz was not on campus, but sent slides of his work. Although Friedman was very interested in Seitz, he decided not to hire anyone at that time.

Early Career Years: New York and Baltimore, 1961–1964

1961–1963 The architectural firm I.M. Pei & Associates hires Seitz. The New York firm pioneered the concept of including a graphic design department within a larger, multidisciplinary practice. Seitz's graphic design projects include work on the graphics and signage for Place Ville Marie in Montreal

Yale University Art Gallery, 2007

as well as the United States Information Agency exhibition *American Production Facilities*.

1962 Bud Leake, a schoolmate of Seitz's from Yale, invites him to interview for a teaching position at the Maryland Institute College of Art (MICA) in Baltimore.

Seitz becomes the third graphic design faculty member at MICA. During his first year there, he teaches the foundation course, beginning graphic design, and photography.

The Walker Art Center Years: Roots of Minnesota Modernism, 1964–1968
1964 Martin Friedman invites Seitz to Minneapolis to interview for a design curator position at the Walker Art Center. He is appointed Walker design curator and editor of *Design Quarterly*, the museum's national publication of applied arts, architecture, and design.

At the Walker, Seitz curates the exhibitions *Toward a New City* (September 17 to October 24, 1965), *Norman Ives: Graphic Design* (August 7 to September 11, 1966), *Furniture by Breuer/Le Corbusier/Mies van der Rohe 1924–1931* (November 21 to December 31, 1966), and *Mass Transit: Problem and Promise* (March 21 to April 28, 1968).

Freelance Exploration, Community Building & InterDesign: An Interdisciplinary Approach to Design, 1968–1978
1968 When the Walker Art Center announces plans to temporarily close in 1969 for construction of its new building designed by Edward Larrabee Barnes, Seitz leaves to start his own graphic design business.

He opens his first graphic design firm, Visual Communication, Inc., as a solo practitioner. Clients include the Guthrie Theater, Hazelden

left: **Peter Seitz, circa 1964**   right: **Martin Friedman, Director of the Walker Art Center, 1962**

Treatment Center, the Minneapolis Public Library, and Carleton College.

1969–1978 Seitz (graphic design), Duane Thorbeck and Alfred French (architecture), Roger B. Martin (landscape architecture), and later Stephen Kahne (computer specialist) launch InterDesign Inc., the Twin Cities' premier interdisciplinary design firm. Its first job is a small urban-planning project for the City of New Ulm, Minnesota. Major projects included identity programs and signage systems for the Minneapolis Parkways, the downtown St. Paul Skyways, the Minnesota State Capital, and the Minnesota Zoological Gardens.

1970 Seitz establishes the first category listing for graphic designers in the Minneapolis/St. Paul Yellow Pages.

Seitz helps organize the Community Design Center (CDC), a design cooperative located at 118 West 26th Street, Minneapolis, which enables local graphic designers and architects to collaborate and provide pro bono work for social causes in the area. Other members of this nonprofit organization's board of directors include architecture notables Roger Clemence, Alfred French, Bob Hysell, Roger B. Martin, Milo Thompson, and Duane Thorbeck.

The first *Print Casebook* series features the signage system for the Minneapolis Parkways.

Teaching 1971–2002
1971 Seitz begins teaching the third-year graphic design course at the Minneapolis College of Art and Design (MCAD).

1976 Seitz attends an organizational meeting at the Design Center of the Minnesota Graphic

Designers Association (MGDA), the first professional organization for graphic designers in Minnesota. Tim Larsen and Dale Johnston become co-chairs of this organizational effort. Seitz explains, "Besides the Art Director's Club, there was no professional design organization to represent graphic designers in the Twin Cities. We were not 'commercial artists' (a term used in the 1950s and 1960s), nor were we advertising designers. The profession of graphic design was a new one and needed a new name."

1977–1978 Seitz holds the position of chair of the design division at MCAD.

1977 MGDA is officially incorporated as a nonprofit Minnesota corporation. Newly elected officers include Jim Johnson (chairman), Eric Madsen (vice chairman/treasurer), and Tim Larsen (secretary). An MGDA press release

announces its officers and goals in a charter Seitz helped to draft.

1978 Seitz is elected chairman of MGDA.

Corporate Identity: Award-Winning Design, 1978–1986
1978–1986 Seitz departs InterDesign to form Seitz Graphic Direction, which includes former InterDesign senior graphic designer Hideki Yamamoto and other members of the studio's graphic design staff.

1980 Seitz Graphic Direction changes its name to Seitz Yamamoto Moss after the three principals—Seitz, Hideki Yamamoto, and Miranda Moss (formerly Pat Seitz). The firm specializes in corporate identity projects. Clients include Lutheran Brotherhood (now Thrivent Financial for Lutherans); Control Data Corporation; Miracle Ear; American

Medical Systems; the State of Minnesota; Hammel, Green and Abrahamson (HGA); Gelco Corporation; and Ellerbe Associates.

1981 Seitz begins assembling one of MCAD's first computer graphics laboratories, which features state-of-the art equipment and dedicated systems for specific design tasks and develops curriculum in this area.

1983–1986 Seitz serves on the American Institute of Graphic Arts (AIGA) National Board of Directors.

1984 Seitz designs the logo, promotional materials, and signage for the SIGGRAPH Conference, which was the largest conference held in Minneapolis up to that time.

The original Macintosh computer is released. MCAD was one of the first art schools to acquire this revolutionary new technology for its computer lab.

1985–1994 He lectures at several art schools and universities in the United States and teaches one month per year at the University of Osaka, Japan.

1986 MGDA elects to affiliate with the national AIGA organization and becomes AIGA Minnesota. To honor his contributions to the Twin Cities design community, Seitz is the first invited speaker at the Insights lecture series, a prestigious annual forum featuring some of the most respected and innovative designers in the world. The lecture series is cosponsored by AIGA Minnesota and the Walker Art Center.

1986–1994 Seitz's new design firm, Peter Seitz & Associates, includes such clients as Ecolab, the Minneapolis Convention Center, and 3M,

left: Graphic design students using a newly acquired computer in the lab at the Minneapolis College of Art and Design, 1984   right: Gala dinner in conjunction with Seitz's AIGA Fellow Award (left to right): Tim Eaton, Peter Seitz, Ric Grefe, and Eric Madsen, 2001

Personnel Decisions, Inc., Edina's Centennial Lakes retail area, the Mayo Clinic, and the Pacifico Convention and Exhibition Center in Yokohama, Japan.

1995–1996 Seitz purchases land in the countryside near Pepin, Wisconsin. He designs and builds his dream home, which is completed in 1996.

1996 Seitz retires from MCAD and receives the title professor emeritus, but continues to teach part-time.

1998–1999 Seitz serves as acting chair of the design department at MCAD.

2000 Seitz is the first Minnesota recipient of the AIGA Fellow Award.

2001–2002 Seitz teaches the critique course in the MFA program at MCAD.

2006 Seitz cofounds the Lake Pepin Art & Design Center in Pepin, Wisconsin.

Seitz's home in rural Wisconsin, 2007

Curriculum Vitae

Peter Seitz
American, b. Germany, 1931

Education
1978 Summer program in computer graphics, Massachusetts Institute of Technology, Cambridge, Massachusetts

1959–1961 Master of Fine Arts in Graphic Design and Photography, Yale University, School of Art, New Haven, Connecticut

1955–1959 Bachelor's degree, diploma in Visual Communication, Hochschule für Gestaltung Ulm, Germany

1954–1955 Studies in graphic design, Kunstschule der Stadt Augsburg

Faculty Appointments
1971–2002 Professor, Program in Graphic Design, Minneapolis College of Art and Design, Minnesota (1971–1982, Assistant and Associate Professor; 1983, Professor; 1996, Professor Emeritus)

1998–1999 Acting Chair, Design Department, Minneapolis College of Art and Design

1977–1978 Chair, Design Department, Minneapolis College of Art and Design

1962–1964 Instructor, Program in Graphic Design, Maryland Institute College of Art, Baltimore

Professional Experience
1986–1994 President, Peter Seitz & Associates, Inc., Minneapolis, Minnesota

1978–1986 President and Creative Director, Seitz Yamamoto Moss, Inc., Minneapolis, Minnesota

1969–1978 Partner and Design Director, InterDesign Inc., Minneapolis, Minnesota

1968–1969 Senior Graphic Designer, Visual Communications, Inc., Minneapolis, Minnesota

1964–1968 Curator of Design and Editor of *Design Quarterly*, Walker Art Center, Minneapolis, Minnesota

1961–1962 Graphic Designer, I.M. Pei and Associates, New York

1960 Art Director, McCann Erickson, Inc., New York

Selected Honors and Awards
Advertising Federation of Minnesota
American Institute of Graphic Arts Fellow, AIGA Minnesota Chapter
Art Directors Club of Baltimore
Art Directors Club of Minneapolis
Art Directors Club of New York
DESI Awards
Graphis Annual
Minnesota Graphic Designers Association
Potlatch Corporation
Print Regional Annual
Society of Environmental Graphic Designers
Society of Publication Designers
Society of Typographic Arts

Selected Clients
Abbott Northwestern Hospital
American Medical Systems
Apache Corporation
Audiotone, Inc.
BBDO
Bethesda Hospital
Capitol Area Architecture and Planning Board
Carleton College
City of Des Moines
City of South St. Paul
Control Data Corporation
CPT Corporation
Dahlberg Electronics
Dayton-Hudson Corporation
Dayton's Department Stores
Duluth Transportation Museum
Ecolab Inc.
Ellerbe Architects, Inc.
Fargo Hospital and Clinic
First Bank Minneapolis
First National Bank of St. Paul
Grain Terminal Association
General Mills
Hammel, Green and Abrahamson
Hennepin County Library Board
Hill and Knowlton
Hazelden Treatment Center
IBM Corporation
Jefferson Buslines
Korsunsky Krank Erickson
Lowertown Development Corporation
Lutheran Brotherhood
Macalester College
Mankato State University
Mayo Clinic
Medtronic
MeritCare, Inc.
Metropolitan Medical Center
Midland Management
Midwest Federal Savings and Loan
Minneapolis Children's Medical Center
Minneapolis College of Art and Design
Minneapolis Convention Center
Minneapolis Institute of Arts
Minneapolis Park Board
Minneapolis Public Libraries
Minneapolis Public Schools
Minneapolis Society of Fine Arts
Minnegasco

Miracle Ear
Minnesota Department of
Agriculture
Minnesota Department of
Natural Resources
Minnesota Graphic Designers
Association
Minnesota Higher Education
Minnesota Historical Society
Minnesota Mutual
Minnesota Opera
Minnesota State Art Council
Minnesota State University
Moorhead
Minnesota Zoo
New Ulm Business Districts, Inc.
Nippon Wilson Learning, Inc.
Northern States Power Company
North Star Financial Corporation
Northwest Architect magazine
Northwestern National Life
Insurance
Oppenheimer Law Firm
Pacifico Convention Center,
Yokohama, Japan
Padilla and Speer
Pillsbury
R2E of America
Saint John's University
Security Financial Bank
SCIMED
SIGGRAPH
Spearhead Industries
Sperry Univac
Spring Hill Conference Center
St. Louis County Historical Society
St. Louis Public Schools System
St. Paul Skyways
State of Minnesota
Stolpestad, Brown and Smith, P.A.
Target
3M Company
Trane Sentinel
U.S. Army Corps of Engineers
U.S. Department of Housing and
Urban Development
U.S. Department of Interior
U.S. Environmental Protection
Agency
U.S. Fish and Wildlife Service

University of Minnesota
Vinland National Center
Walker Art Center
Wilson Learning, Inc.
Yale University Press

Publications Edited by Peter Seitz
Design and Planning 2: Computers
in Design and Communications,
Martin Krampen and Peter
Seitz, eds. (New York: Hastings
House, 1967).
Design Quarterly 61: The 13th
Triennale, 1964
Design Quarterly 62: Signs and
Symbols in Graphic
Communication, 1965
Design Quarterly 63: "A Clip-On
Architecture", 1965
Design Quarterly 64: Dynamics
of Shape, 1966
Design Quarterly 65: Bruno
Mathsson: Furniture/Structures/
Ideas, 1966
Design Quarterly 66/67: Design
and the Computer, 1966
Design Quarterly 68: Design
and Light, 1967
Design Quarterly 69/70: The
Expression of Gio Ponti, 1967
Design Quarterly 71:
Mass Transit: Problems
and Promise, 1968
Design Quarterly 72: Toward
the Future, 1968

Selected Writings, Articles,
and Reviews
Articles by and about Peter Seitz
have been featured in such
publications as Architecture
Minnesota, Computer User,
Designcourse, IDEA Magazine
(Japan), Portfolio (Japan), Print,
and XPLOR magazine.

Altman, Peter. "Walker Showing
Dramatizes Potential of Mass
Transit." Minneapolis Star,
March 22, 1968.

"Centennial Logo." ARTs magazine,
Minneapolis Institute of Arts
(November 1982), n.p.
"Computers for Artists and
Designers." Portfolio (October–
November 1986): 43–45.
"Corporate Identity: From 11
Vantage Points." STA Design
Journal (February 1985): 30–33.
Cunningham, Dick. "Community
Center Nears Completion."
Minneapolis Tribune,
June 12, 1967.
"Graphic Design in Architecture."
Architecture Minnesota
(July–August 1979): 42–45.
Herring, Jerry. The Art and
Business of Creative Self-
Promotion (New York: Watson
Guptill, 1987).
"Minnesota." Print (July/August
1981): 98–99.
Morrison, Don. "Transit Exhibit
Warns Cities to Get Moving."
Minneapolis Star, March 28,
1968.
Probst, Alison and Robert.
"Interview." Design Journal 1:3
(1983): 2–4.
Seitz, Peter. "Graphic Directions on
the Computer." Design
Journal 1:1(1983): 4–7.
_____. "Peter Seitz." Designcourse
1:2 (Summer 1969): 36–37.
Steele, Mike. "Gallery for Design—
the Total City." Minneapolis
Tribune, March 17, 1968, Home
and Recreation 1, 14.
Winegar, Karin. "Signer of
Our Times." Star Tribune,
August 27, 1997.

Afterword

Andrew Blauvelt, Design Director
and Curator, Walker Art Center

A few years ago, I received a set of two small booklets
documenting the work of Gene and Jackie Lacy, a husband
and wife team that operated a design firm in Indianapolis
from the early 1950s through the 1970s. Having lived and
studied graphic design in Indianapolis, I knew the names
and recognized some of the designs, but I'm sure that was
not the case for the majority of people who received this
publication—particularly those without a connection to the
city. A letter attached to this mailing offered some insights into
its purpose: "Gene and Jackie Lacy worked as graphic designers,
illustrators and artists in Indianapolis from the 1950s through
the 1990s—four decades spent creating a substantial body
of work that with few exceptions, remains virtually unknown
outside a small group of family and friends. . . . The Lacys were
not widely known beyond Indianapolis and like so many of their
contemporaries, may never be recognized for their contributions
to graphic design. Hopefully, this modest mailing goes some
distance to rectify that oversight. Although numerous graphic
design magazines regularly profile contemporary designers
and their predecessors, I am unaware of any national or regional
efforts to document and preserve the work of people like the
Lacys. In many cases this lesser known work is vanishing bit
by bit every day."[1]

As both a graphic designer and a design curator, I was
immediately drawn to this project and the questions it raises:
Who "counts" as history, where are we looking, and how do

1. Letter accompanying the
publication *Commercial Article*
(Indianapolis, Indiana: Commercial
Artisan, 2005).

we "preserve" it? While the history of graphic design is not limited to its practitioners, the hard work of expanding the canon—designer by designer—remains largely undone. It is rare to encounter a newly unearthed designer and far more common to see new interpretations of established figures. Although there are multiple reasons for this, I believe that one of the major difficulties is attributable to the very complicated, typically unpaid, and investigative nature of such primary historical work. This kind of work entails hundreds of hours of painstaking research—trying to locate actual examples of projects, tracking down former colleagues, and, when possible, gaining an individual's trust and thus attaining access to a living subject's archives and recollections, all of which require negotiating the complexities of having to evaluate someone's career and impact.

In the case of the Lacys, this work was undertaken as a kind of labor of love—the story written by one of their daughters and the piece designed and published by their son-in-law, James Sholly at Commercial Artisan. Most often, I would venture to say, such undertakings are projects of passion—the enthusiasm that drives the endeavor resides in spouses, family members, former colleagues, students, and business partners. The story presented here is really no different, as the acknowledgments and contributions throughout can attest. Personally, I also have a direct connection to the work of Peter Seitz—our common history as design directors and curators at the Walker Art Center in Minneapolis. Although more than thirty years separate our respective tenures at the Walker, there is an inherent commonality in the shared experiences, challenges, and opportunities that such a position offers. I was struck by Peter's recollections of his time at the Walker and could easily relate to the harried nature of the job's demands, although I'm not a staff of one! Peter was one of the first designers in Minneapolis to visit me when I came to town. Unfortunately, I did not know much about him and his experience at the Walker or his career in the Twin Cities, for that matter. However, I did leave our meeting with a renewed curiosity about design at the museum "before Mickey," a reference to Mildred Friedman, the Walker's legendary former design curator and editor of *Design Quarterly*, who succeeded Peter in 1968 and whose projects cemented the Walker's already outsized reputation in the world of design. This publication and my contributions to it are but a small gesture toward the larger debt of gratitude that I and the current and future design staffs at the Walker owe to people like Peter, who not only demonstrated a commitment to modern design but made it a reality in both theory and practice.

The professionalization of graphic design in the United States—the transformation of what was a rather ad hoc combination of typesetters, jobbing printers, and so-called "advertising" and "commercial artists," who learned their crafts essentially on the job, into a more clearly defined career that one could be schooled in—is a story closely aligned with the importation, adaptation, and dissemination of European modernism in the United States. The principles of modern graphic design—the favoring of sans-serif typefaces; the use of grid systems to order texts and images on the page; the focus on processes, systems, and methods to generate solutions to problems; the belief in a shared visual language that could be learned and manipulated; and the privileging of "content" over "persuasion"—insured its potency as something that can be disseminated broadly. The fusion of these characteristics held sway most deeply in the realm of modern postwar corporate identities (the precursor of branding). As a testament to its dominance in the field worldwide, design historian Philip Meggs dubbed it the "International Typographic Style." Peter Seitz had a particularly important trajectory in his life—his studies at such legendary schools as HfG Ulm and Yale with teachers such as Max Bill, Otl Aicher, Paul Rand, Alvin Eisenman, Bradbury Thompson, Herbert Matter, and so on—which would eventually lead him, as a first generation disciple of postwar modernism, to Minnesota at the correct historical moment for such ideas to take hold. His shepherding of younger designers and his own turn as a teacher at the Minneapolis College of Art and Design would further inculcate these values in newer generations. In fact, the influence of modernism seems strongest as it courses through classrooms and studios. Katherine McCoy, a designer and educator at Cranbrook Academy of Art and later the Institute of Design at the Illinois Institute of Technology, has recently undertaken chronicling the histories of modern graphic design programs in the United States, the Kansas City Art Institute and the Philadelphia College of Art (now University of the Arts) in particular.[2] It is not surprising, perhaps, that as these stories unfold, we find a thicket of connections as well as new branches to explore. If this work is "vanishing bit by bit," there is a renewed sense of urgency to document the lives of graphic designers who were so influential in the formation and maturation of the field in their respective cities.

The larger question that these historical projects pose is a broader historical one: how did modern design spread across the United States? The answers can help us create a more intricate and detailed picture of graphic design history, focusing long-overdue attention on local practitioners—pioneers whose work helped pave the way for other contemporary practices. Conventional histories of graphic design are focused on designers from the northeastern United States (specifically New York City and vicinity) and California (Los Angeles, in particular), with an occasional nod to the Midwest represented by Chicago. This geographic triangulation creates a hierarchy that ignores what is a more realistic dispersal pattern across the United States—the serendipitous arrival of new ideas and practices of modern design in far-flung places between the coasts. It is fitting therefore that Peter's work was featured in the first issue of *Print* magazine's *Regional Annual* of 1981, one of the profession's first acknowledgments of the decentralization of graphic design—a testament to the growing influence beyond

2. Katherine McCoy has researched the role of Rob Roy Kelly (an alumnus of the Minneapolis School of Art, the precursor of MCAD), who established a new graphic design program at the Kansas City Art Institute in the 1960s. Like Peter Seitz, he received his MFA in design from Yale University and worked at the Walker Art Center. See her essay "Bits and Pieces of Basel," *Print* magazine (March/April 2005): 45–51.

the coasts. It noted that "design in Minnesota is characterized by a kind of indefinable stateliness. . . . its clean edges and bright colors reveal a rational choice for content over style. . . . the influence is Swiss." [3]

This is not necessarily about writing History with a capital *H*, but rather what has been termed "history from below," a reference to the grassroots nature of the work, its decentralized locations, oral histories, and marginalized subjects. It is a term and concept that should be embraced rather than shunned, because the groundwork of history and the field it supports has its foundation in this low-lying metaphor. The story of Peter Seitz provides one answer to this question, one more piece of a bigger puzzle. We can rest assured that there are many more stories such as his in cities across the country—"modernism in the fly-over zone," as I once half-jokingly described it. Hopefully, this project can be greater than the sum of its parts by acting as a prototype and catalyst for other stories waiting to be told. The hard work of history has only just begun.

3. *Print's Regional Design Annual* (July/August 1981): 98.

Photography and Reproduction Credits

Peter Seitz
Designing a Life

First Edition ©2007 The Minneapolis College of Art & Design

Designers Andrew Blauvelt, Ryan Nelson
Editors Andrew Blauvelt, Pamela Johnson
Publication Manager Pam Arnold
Image Production Greg Beckel

Printed in Minneapolis, Minnesota, at Shapco Printing.

Library of Congress Cataloging-in-Publication Data available
upon request.

ISBN 978-0-9800893-0-1